One Great Cloud of Witnesses!

You and Your Congregation
in the Evangelical Lutheran Church in America

A Guide to Our Life Together in Mission

by Lowell G. Almen

Augsburg Fortress
Minneapolis

ONE GREAT CLOUD OF WITNESSES!
You and Your Congregation in the Evangelical Lutheran Church in America,
Third Edition

Cover design: David Meyer
Cover photo: St. Philip's Lutheran Church steeple, Fridley, Minn., by Pastor Leslie G. Svendsen.

The Library of Congress has cataloged the first edition as follows:
Almen, Lowell G., 1941–
One great cloud of witnesses! : you and your congregation in the
Evangelical Lutheran Church in America / by Lowell G. Almen.
   p. cm.
"A guide to our life together in mission."
Includes bibliographical references.
ISBN 0-8066-3622-X (alk. paper)
1. Evangelical Lutheran Church in America. 2. Lutheran Church—History.
I. Title.
   BX8048.3.A64   1997
   284.1'35—dc21
                                      97-19707
                                         CIP

Third Edition ISBNs:
ISBN-13: 978-0-8066-3853-9
ISBN-10: 0-8066-3853-2

One Great Cloud of Witnesses!

Contents

Introduction

As One of Many

We are sitting in worship. The lector is reading the Second Lesson for the day from Romans 12: "For as in one body we have many members, and not all the members have the same function, so we, who are many, are one body in Christ. . . ." The reader continues: "Let love be genuine. . . . Rejoice in hope. . . . Contribute to the needs of the saints . . . " (Romans 12:4, 5, 9, 12, and 13). The words linger in our hearing, "So we . . . are one body"—the body of Christ, the church.

As members of the Evangelical Lutheran Church in America (ELCA), we confess that we are one part of that larger body of Christ, the church.

Given our commitments and concerns, you or I may have asked at some point the questions, "What is happening in the Evangelical Lutheran Church in America?" and "Where do I fit into such a big church?" Answers to such broad but crucial questions may not be simple ones. Yet we can find easily at least part of the response. To do so, we can look into a mirror and repeat our inquiry.

After all, the members of the Evangelical Lutheran Church in America are "the baptized members of its congregations." When we want to know what is happening in the ELCA, you and I must look at ourselves to answer, at least partially, our own questions.

To provide a thorough answer, we would need to survey all 4.9 million other baptized members of ELCA congregations. We would have to examine the witness and work of each of the ELCA's 10,500 congregations. We would be required to study the ministry of each of the ELCA's 65 synods. Then we would have to comprehend the broad scope of the domestic and international mission that we share through our churchwide ministries.

That is the aim of this book. It may not give all the answers that some may seek. Indeed, it is not a summary of a survey of members. Nor is it an historical account of each congregation. Instead it is an overview of what unites us as Lutherans and of what we do together as members of the Evangelical Lutheran Church in America.

Toward the end of the twentieth century, major ecumenical developments occurred. Many of these reflected the reception of the results of decades of dialogue. For example, on October 31, 1999, the *Joint Declaration on the Doctrine of Justification* was signed by representatives of the Lutheran World Federation and the Roman Catholic Church at Augsburg, Germany. The Evangelical Lutheran Church in America also entered into agreements of "full communion," or official mutual recognition, with several churches. These opened the way for cooperation in mission efforts in strategic settings.

The purpose of this book is to help you become better acquainted with our church, with the basics of the faith we confess, with our shared mission, and with the heritage that we cherish. It is intended for both new and long-term members of ELCA congregations, and particularly for members of congregation councils and other congregational and synodical leaders.

As secretary of the Evangelical Lutheran Church in America since its beginning in 1987, I have had almost daily contact with the many aspects of our church's life and work. Through this position as a churchwide officer and through service in a predecessor church body, I have come in touch with church life both throughout this nation and elsewhere in the world.

From that knowledge and experience, I invite you on this journey with me, a journey of thought, discovery, and reflection. We will find, much to our delight, that we are part of a beautiful Lutheran tapestry of faith, commitment, and service.

THE REVEREND LOWELL G. ALMEN
All Saints' Day ✜ November 1, 2006

1

Between Heritage and Hope

THE EARTH MOVED

When the Evangelical Lutheran Church in America (ELCA) was being formed, the earth moved. Not by much. Not for long. And few people noticed—for good reason.

It happened only days after the opening of what would become the ELCA's churchwide office in Chicago. On Wednesday, June 10, 1987, a moderate earthquake was felt in Chicago at 6:49 P.M. The quake measured 5.0 on the Richter scale and lasted only 15 seconds.

The epicenter of the quake was some distance from Chicago, near Lawrenceville, Illinois, in the southern part of the state. But its rumbling was felt in 15 midwestern states.

Obviously, the earthquake had no relation to the organizing of a churchwide office in Chicago. Symbolically, however, the event—little noticed by most people and forgotten by nearly all—foreshadowed the major changes that were to come.

YOUNG YET OLD

The constituting assembly for the newly forming Evangelical Lutheran Church in America had ended on May 3, 1987. What occurred in succeeding months marked a time of gigantic change for the landscape of Lutheranism throughout the United States and the Caribbean region.

On January 1, 1988, the Evangelical Lutheran Church in America (ELCA) officially began operation. Thus, the ELCA became the younger of the two large Lutheran churches in North America; the other one, The Lutheran Church–Missouri Synod, was established in 1847. The ELCA, however, also may be considered the oldest U.S. Lutheran church body, tracing its history through its predecessors to the mid-1600s in the area now known as New York. Early Lutheran development occurred elsewhere, too, as a result of immigration.

To illustrate, the ten oldest congregations in the Evangelical Lutheran Church in America are (by order of age):

1. 1649: First Lutheran Church, Albany, New York
2. 1666: Frederick Evangelical Lutheran Church, Charlotte Amalie, St. Thomas, U.S. Virgin Islands
3. 1700: New Hanover Lutheran Church, New Hanover, Pennsylvania
4. 1703: Zion Lutheran Church, Athens, New York
5. 1710: Christ Lutheran Church, Germantown, New York
6. 1710: St. Paul Lutheran Church, West Camp, New York
7. 1714: Zion Lutheran Church, Oldwick, New Jersey
8. 1715: St. Paul Lutheran Church, Red Hook, New York
9. 1715: St. John Lutheran Church, Manorton, New York
10. 1715: Christ Lutheran Church, Suffern Airmont, New York[1]

MAJOR STEP TOWARD UNITY

The ELCA was created by the uniting of the 2.85 million-member Lutheran Church in America (LCA), the 2.25 million-member American Lutheran Church (ALC), and the 100,000-member Association of Evangelical Lutheran Churches (AELC).[2]

For those fascinated with minute detail, it can be noted that at precisely 12:01 A.M. (Central Standard Time) on January 1, 1988, in accord with the articles for merger, the ELCA became the surviving corporation into which were merged the corporations of the ALC, LCA, and AELC.

Intense efforts to form the ELCA began in 1982 when the three uniting churches made a commitment to come together. To fulfill that commitment, the three churches in their conventions elected a commission of 70 people to draft the constitution and other documents for this new church. Even that significant step had been preceded by many years of cooperative efforts. It also reflected the long-held dream of numerous members and leaders for greater Lutheran unity.

Only four years later, in August 1986, the conventions of the three uniting churches approved the ELCA's constitution, articles of merger, and other documents. Then came the historic moment of the ELCA's constituting assembly, held April 30 through May 3, 1987, in Columbus, Ohio.

In the weeks that followed, the ELCA's 65 synods formally were organized. Synodical bishops and other officers were elected. Offices for several of those synods used facilities that had been synodical or district offices in the predecessor church bodies. Other synods had to establish offices in new places, just as was the case for the churchwide office.

But the basic "expression" of the ELCA—namely, each congregation—continued worship and ministry with little change. Like the largely forgotten June 10, 1987, Illinois earthquake, few members—unless they had particular interest in church administration—noticed the changes that were taking place beyond each congregation. Intense planning and major effort, however, went into creating the respective ELCA synods and establishing a new ELCA churchwide office.

The ELCA united into one church body members in congregations located throughout the 50 U.S. states and in Puerto Rico and the Virgin Islands.

LARGE—FOR A PURPOSE

The ELCA's membership is geographically widespread—from St. Croix in the Virgin Islands to the Seward Peninsula in Alaska. Heaviest concentrations of ELCA members, however, are found in a half-moon stretching from the Dakotas and Minnesota, at one point, around the Great Lakes into Pennsylvania and adjacent states, at the other point.

Total membership of the ELCA is equivalent to the combined populations of Los Angeles and Philadelphia. Or, to describe the ELCA's size another way, the total membership is equal to the combined populations of Minnesota and North Dakota.

The state with the largest number of ELCA members is Minnesota (838,941 in 2005). The state with the greatest number of ELCA congregations is Pennsylvania (1,300).

If you or I had set out in the year 2001, at the start of the twenty-first century, to worship in a different ELCA congregation each Sunday, we would still be worshiping in a different congregation throughout the first decade of the twenty-third century. Some 211 years would be required to complete the circuit. Even visiting for only a day in each congregation, seven days a week, would take 30 years.

The ELCA, however, is not a big church for the sake of being large. This church's size is an opportunity. Through it, you and I are united in a shared faith and summoned to a shared mission.

We, as members of the ELCA, live between heritage and hope. We draw on the rich heritage of our church, a heritage that arises directly from the Lutheran Reformation of the sixteenth century and from the whole apostolic tradition of the church. At the same time, our heritage calls us into active participation in the larger community of the whole church of Jesus Christ. As participants in the one holy catholic and apostolic church and as members of the ELCA, we live in God-given hope nourished by the gospel. We seek to serve in the God-given mission to go into all the world and make disciples of every nation (Matthew 28:18-20).

2

New but Old

WHERE DO WE FIT IN?

Of the 5.8 billion people in the world, 1.9 billion are Christians, 1.1 billion are followers of Islam, 800 million are Hindus, 300 million are Buddhists, 13.5 million are Jews, and the rest are scattered among several other religions or are avowed atheists.

More than half of the Christian population are Roman Catholics, who account for 1.1 billion people. The Orthodox number 175 million people and the Anglicans, 78 million people.

The number of Lutherans worldwide exceeds 69 million people. Of that total, 66 million belong to the 140 member churches of the Lutheran World Federation.

The 6.9 million-member Church of Sweden is the largest of the member churches of the Lutheran World Federation (LWF). The Evangelical Lutheran Church in America (ELCA) is second in size (4.9 million) but largest in terms of active membership. The third largest LWF member church is the Evangelical Lutheran Church of Finland with 4.6 million members.

Germany, where the Lutheran heritage was born in the Reformation era, has the largest number of Lutherans in any one country. Its regionally based Lutheran churches have a combined membership of 13 million, followed by the 8.1 million Lutherans in North America.

Other large Lutheran populations are found in Denmark (4.5 million), Ethiopia (4.3 million), Norway (3.9 million), Indonesia (3.8 million), Tanzania (3.5 million), India (1.6 million), Madagascar (1.5 million), Nigeria (1.4 million), Namibia (1.1 million), and Brazil (712,000).

WITHIN NORTH AMERICA

While ELCA members account for 4.9 million of the 8.1 million
Lutherans in North America, the second largest Lutheran church
body on this continent is the St. Louis-based Lutheran Church–
Missouri Synod (LCMS) with 2.4 million members. Third in size
with 400,000 members is the Wisconsin Evangelical Lutheran
Synod (WELS), based in Milwaukee. Some 271,000 Lutherans live
in Canada; of that number nearly 188,000 belong to the Evangelical Lutheran Church in Canada, which historically is closely
related to the ELCA. The rest of the Lutherans in North America
are scattered throughout about a dozen smaller groups, some with
fewer than 500 members. Of the smaller groups, the largest is the
39,000-member Association of Free Lutheran Congregations,
headquartered in suburban Minneapolis.

Of the Christian church bodies in the United States of America,
the Evangelical Lutheran Church in America is listed as sixth in size:

1. Roman Catholic Church—68 million
2. Southern Baptist Convention—16.3 million
3. United Methodist Church—8.1 million
4. Church of God in Christ—5.5 million
5. National Baptist Convention U.S.A.—estimated 5 million
6. Evangelical Lutheran Church in America—4.9 million

Other large U. S. church bodies include: National Baptist Convention of America, 3.5 million; Presbyterian Church (U.S.A.),
3.1 million; African Methodist Episcopal Church, 2.5 million; The
Lutheran Church–Missouri Synod, as noted above, 2.4 million;
and The Episcopal Church, 2.3 million.

WHAT'S IN A NAME?

Perhaps a mistake was made in the name given to the 70-member
group that was elected to form the ELCA. The group, chosen by
the 1982 conventions of the three uniting churches, was desig-
nated as the Commission for a New Lutheran Church (CNLC).[1]
The selection of that name was deliberate; it was chosen as a signal
of a common coming together of the once separate church bodies.
The desire was to avoid an appearance of a negotiated merger in
which various parts of the "old" uniting churches would be pieced

together in give-and-take debates and compromises. Therefore, the "commission of seventy," as it sometimes was called, was given the task of creating a "new" church, not merely a merging of the structures, patterns, practices, and programs of the "old" churches.

All of the talk about a "new" church raised concerns among some members in congregations of the uniting churches; it also fostered false expectations among others. To some, a "new" church implied casting aside everything that they had known and held precious in their Lutheran heritage and in their particular church body. To others, "new" church suggested nothing was nailed down, everything was up for negotiation, and anything would go—until the "new" church decided for itself what teachings, standards, and commitments would apply in the ELCA.

In reality, the history, heritage, standards, programs, commitments, and practices of the three predecessor church bodies— which contained within them all of the threads of Lutheranism in North America—were being woven together into a new tapestry. What members had treasured and held dear in the lives of their own congregations and their own churches was carried forward and grafted into the life of the new church.

The formation of the ELCA represented the grand fulfillment of decades and even centuries of prayer and effort by our Lutheran forebears in the search for greater Lutheran unity. At the same time, there were problems. Some of those difficulties arose from getting new patterns to work; others emerged from a loss of memory with the retirement or shift in work by veteran synodical and churchwide staff persons.

In spite of the anxiety and uncertainty that some saw in those early days, coming together in the ELCA was a moment of joy for many members of the uniting churches. For many years, the question for them had not been, "Why unite?" but rather, "Why not unite—and the sooner the better!" So the commitment that was made in 1982 by the conventions of The American Lutheran Church, Association of Evangelical Lutheran Churches, and Lutheran Church in America was a sign of great promise. The three church bodies agreed to "commit themselves to join in forming a new Lutheran church and to take all deliberate steps toward its earliest realization."[2]

After the ELCA was established in 1987, an ongoing challenge was to understand, on the one hand, the degree of unity needed to remain as a united church and, on the other hand, the amount of diversity that could exist to reflect the differing patterns of church life, particularly those that are regional, local, or historical in character. Furthermore, even in the same community, differences could be found in the practices and styles of ELCA congregations.

Experience demonstrated that the ELCA was both a "new" and an "old" church. It was "new" in the sense of being young; "new" in bringing together so many members, congregations, synods, and churchwide ministries into one church body; "new" in looking toward the future in the God-given mission that was set before this church. Yet the ELCA also was an "old" church, part of the whole tradition of the church of Jesus Christ and part of the particular communion of churches of the Lutheran Reformation. It also reflected a weaving together of distinctive Lutheran histories contained within its predecessor church bodies. Yes, "new," but we are a church with solid foundations. Yes, "old," but we also are a church with an eye toward a future blessed by God as we ELCA members together seek to be faithful, individually and collectively, in witness and service.

EVANGELICAL AT THE CORE

When Martin Luther sought to debate key Christian principles, he posted on October 31, 1517, his 95 theses on the church door at Wittenberg. It was a university town. The church door was the common bulletin board. He sought discussion of the points he was raising. Yet in that list of 95 statements can be found the core convictions of the "evangelical" movement that would soon emerge. He declared in thesis number 62: "The true treasure of the church is the most holy Gospel of the glory and grace of God."

When a name was being proposed for the new Lutheran church, the word *evangelical* was suggested for several reasons. Its roots are in the Greek word for "gospel." The name has been employed since the Reformation to identify those who emphasize the doctrine of justification by grace through faith and the authority of Scripture in the life of both the whole church and individual believers. It was the name chosen for what was then the newly merged Evangelical Lutheran Church in Canada. Further, it was noted that the name *evangelical* has been widely used by Lutherans in Europe, Africa, South America, Japan, and elsewhere. The name in some places is employed even without the word *Lutheran* because it is seen as the primary designation and identity of Lutherans.

Evangelical was the name preferred by Luther for the movement he led. He thought such a name pointed to the proclamation of the gospel "as the source of the church's life and the living, powerful, creative force through which people are called to faith and sustained in the communion of saints." The word *evangelical* also carries with it an emphasis on mission. "We are called to go into all the world to proclaim the Gospel so that all people may know Christ's love."[3]

The word *Lutheran* was seen as essential in the American context because it underscores our heritage as part of Luther's reform movement. *Lutheran* is the "shorthand" name by which most Lutherans in North America identify themselves.

Interesting elements related to the choice of a name were these facts: Of the 254 Lutheran church bodies in the world in 1985, 239 included the name of their location or country, 198 were identified as "Lutheran" in their name, and 149 also used "evangelical" in their name.

Reflecting our focus on the gospel as the power of God for salvation (in the use of "Evangelical"), respecting our particular heritage within the whole church (with "Lutheran"), and acknowledging the primary arena of our work ("in America"), we identify ourselves as members of the Evangelical Lutheran Church in America.

3

As the Household of the Baptized

THE FAITH WE CONFESS

We are united by a bond that is stronger than family loyalty, deep friendship, common interest, ethnic identity, or national allegiance. This bond is not a human category defined by social context. It is God-given and God-blest.

We confess one faith. As the faithful baptized, we gather in community to worship and be nourished by the Word and sacraments. We are empowered and sent by Christ into daily life as witnesses to the faith in every aspect of our lives. We are Christ's and therefore serve as ambassadors of Christ's church in our homes and in the neighborhoods where we live, in our places of work and recreation, and even in the various arenas of commerce, community life, and government.

The basic summary of what we believe, teach, and confess as Lutherans is contained in chapter 2 of the churchwide constitution of the Evangelical Lutheran Church in America (ELCA), chapter 4 of the ELCA Constitution for Synods, and chapter 2 of the Model Constitution for Congregations of the ELCA. Exactly the same text appears in all three constitutions. We declare together:

1. **Triune God:** This church confesses the Triune God, Father, Son, and Holy Spirit.
2. **Revealed in Jesus Christ:** This church confesses Jesus Christ as Lord and Savior and the Gospel as the power of God for the salvation of all who believe.

a. *As Word Incarnate:* Jesus Christ is the Word of God incarnate, through whom everything was made and through whose life, death, and resurrection God fashions a new creation.

b. *Proclaimed in Law and Gospel:* The proclamation of God's message to us as both Law and Gospel is the Word of God, revealing judgment and mercy through word and deed, beginning with the Word in creation, continuing in the history of Israel, and centering in all its fullness in the person and work of Jesus Christ.

c. *Written Witness to Revelation in Jesus:* The canonical Scriptures of the Old and New Testament are the written Word of God. Inspired by God's Spirit speaking through their authors, they record and announce God's revelation centering in Jesus Christ. Through them God's Spirit speaks to us to create and sustain Christian faith and fellowship for service in the world.

3. **Scripture as Source and Norm:** This church accepts the canonical Scriptures of the Old and New Testaments as the inspired Word of God and the authoritative source and norm of its proclamation, faith, and life.

4. **Ecumenical Creeds Embraced with Whole Church:** This church accepts the Apostles', Nicene, and Athanasian Creeds as true declarations of the faith of this church.

5. **United in Lutheran Witness:** This church accepts the Unaltered Augsburg Confession as a true witness to the Gospel, acknowledging as one with it in faith and doctrine all churches that likewise accept the teachings of the Unaltered Augsburg Confession.

6. **Other Lutheran Writings Accepted:** This church accepts the other confessional writings in the Book of Concord, namely, the Apology of the Augsburg Confession, the Smalcald Articles and the Treatise, the Small Catechism, the Large Catechism, and the Formula of Concord, as further valid interpretations of the faith of the Church.

7. **Gospel as God's Power at Work in the World:** This church confesses the Gospel, recorded in the Holy Scriptures and confessed in the ecumenical creeds and

Lutheran confessional writings, as the power of God to create and sustain the Church for God's mission in the world.[1]

Confessing the name of the one, true God, you and I as members of the ELCA—with all others throughout our church—identify the ELCA with the one, holy, catholic, and apostolic church in the whole world and throughout all ages.

In our declaration of faith in the triune God, we immediately become specific in how God has been revealed most clearly to the church—namely, in Jesus Christ. We learn of this faith through the preaching and teaching of the revealed Word and the witness of the written Scripture of the Old and New Testaments. We declare this faith with other Christians in the confession of the creeds of the whole church.

OUR SPECIFIC HERITAGE

We Lutherans trace our specific heritage to the reformer, Martin Luther. Luther was born on November 10, 1483, in Eisleben, Germany. Much of his life was spent as a professor and pastor in Wittenberg. He died on February 18, 1546. During his 63 years of life and work, the face of Christianity was irrevocably altered.

Luther and the other leaders of the Lutheran Reformation in the sixteenth century did not set out to divide the Western church. Rather, they sought reform. The reform was aimed at renewing the church and refocusing its life, ministry, and service on the proclamation of the gospel—that is, on a faithful witness to God's grace through which we are forgiven. Indeed, the gospel announces that we have been embraced by God through the life, suffering, death, and resurrection of Jesus Christ. Therefore, we are adopted by grace through faith to live as God's people.

In their efforts at reform, Luther and others anchored their efforts in Scripture while maintaining allegiance to the basic tradition of the church, expressed most succinctly in the three ecumenical creeds. They saw the reform movement, therefore, as part of "apostolic succession"—that is, in continuity with the teaching of Christ's apostles. This meant for them, and means for us, that as Christians we are linked to Christ's apostles through faith, and that our community is connected to the whole church throughout the ages.

THE FAITH IN WHICH WE BAPTIZE

The three ecumenical creeds—the Apostles' Creed, the Nicene Creed, and the Athanasian Creed—are accepted by the Evangelical Lutheran Church in America. These statements of faith (*creed* is from the Latin word *credo*, that is, "I believe") have been embraced by Christians throughout the centuries.

The simplest and most straightforward of the ecumenical creeds is the Apostles' Creed. Although it bears the name Apostles' Creed, it was not written by the apostles of the New Testament era. It expresses, however, the essence of the apostolic faith. In its early forms, this creed is the oldest of the three ecumenical creeds. Its content stretches back to about A.D. 150 in the questions that were addressed to candidates for Baptism. The creed itself began to gain its basic form by the third century.

The Apostles' Creed is confessed in Baptism. In its succinct way, it declares the source of faith and the way we are grafted into the body of Christ, the church. As Martin Luther explained in the Small Catechism:

> I believe that God has created me together with all creatures. God has given me and still preserves my body and soul: eyes, ears, and all limbs and senses; reason and all mental faculties. In addition, God daily and abundantly provides . . . all the necessities and nourishment for this body and life. . . . For all of this I owe it to God to thank and praise, serve and obey him. . . .[2]

> I believe that Jesus Christ, true God . . . , and also true human being . . . , is my Lord. He has redeemed me, a lost and con-demned person. He has purchased and freed me from all sins. . . . He has done all this in order that I may belong to him. . . .[3]

> I believe that by my own understanding or strength I cannot believe in Jesus Christ my Lord or come to him, but instead the Holy Spirit has called me through the Gospel, enlightened me with his gifts, made me holy, and kept me in the true faith, just as he calls, gathers, enlightens, and makes holy the whole Christian church on earth and keeps it with Jesus Christ in the one com-mon, true faith.[4]

The Nicene Creed is embraced by churches in both the Eastern and Western traditions. As a result, it is seen as the most universal of the creeds. At Nicaea, near what was then known as Constantinople and now as Istanbul in modern Turkey, church leaders and theologians gathered in A.D. 325 for the Council of Nicaea. They met upon the prompting of the newly converted Constantine, who ruled the Roman Empire. The final form of this creed emerged only after several decades of debate. The earlier text was substantially revised and was endorsed in A.D. 381 by the Council of Constantinople. That later, more orthodox, version gradually became permanent and was in widespread use by the early sixth century.

Not nearly as well known as the Apostles' Creed and the Nicene Creed, the Athanasian Creed, nonetheless, is one that Lutherans acknowledge with other churches. This creed carries the name of a bishop of Alexandria in Egypt, Athanasius, who served during the fourth century. The text of the creed itself, however, is similar to writings of St. Augustine, who was bishop of Hippo in northern Africa in the early fifth century. Quotations from Ambrose, bishop of Milan and vigorous opponent of heresy in the fourth century, also may be found in this creed.

The Athanasian Creed is much longer than the other two ecumenical creeds. Its content also is more theologically complicated; yet it offers a thorough summary of the Christian confession of the triune God and the incarnation. "Now this is the catholic faith," we confess in the Athanasian Creed. "We worship one God in trinity and the Trinity in unity, neither confusing the persons nor dividing the divine being. . . ."[5]

Luther and the other reformers embraced the Athanasian Creed, although they focused to a greater degree with the rest of the church on the more commonly used Apostles' Creed and Nicene Creed.

AUGSBURG CONFESSION—OLD BUT CONTEMPORARY

The Augsburg Confession is the one basic document that defines and unites Lutherans throughout the world. It was the first of a series of "confessional writings" to emerge from the Lutheran Reformation. Its intent was to unite, not divide.

Not only church life but also political history was shaped by the Augsburg Confession. As the principal written "symbol" of the Lutheran church, it expresses the consensus of a body of believers. It reflects the response of faith by the power of God's Spirit to the gospel of reconciliation and forgiveness. It remains the fundamental declaration of the evangelical (that is, gospel-centered) faith of the Lutheran church.

A key understanding of the unity of the whole church is reflected in Article VII of the Augsburg Confession: "Our churches . . . teach that one holy church is to continue forever. The church is the assembly of saints in which the Gospel is taught purely and the sacraments are administered rightly. For the true unity of the church it is enough to agree concerning the teaching of the Gospel and the administration of the sacraments. . . ."[6]

The core of the evangelical faith is expressed in Article IV on justification: "It is also taught among us that we cannot obtain forgiveness of sin and righteousness before God by our own merits, works, or satisfactions, but that we receive forgiveness of sin and become righteous before God by grace, for Christ's sake, through faith, when we believe that Christ suffered for us and that for his sake our sin is forgiven and righteousness and eternal life are given to us. . . ."[7]

This gift of faith does not come by accident or personal self-discovery. Rather, God uses particular means to embrace and claim us. As declared in Article V on the ministry of the church: "In order that we may obtain this faith, the ministry of teaching the Gospel and administering the sacraments was instituted. For through the Word and the sacraments, as through instruments, the Holy Spirit is given, and the Holy Spirit produces faith, where and when it pleases God, in those who hear the Gospel. That is to say, it is not on account of our own merits but on account of Christ that God justifies those who believe that they are received into favor for Christ's sake."[8]

Declaration of the church's trinitarian faith and statements on the Lutheran understanding of Baptism, the Lord's Supper, original sin, confession, repentance, faith and good works, and church order are found in the Augsburg Confession. Descriptions of theological and liturgical abuses that needed correction also are provided.

HOW IT CAME TO BE WRITTEN

The Augsburg Confession emerged from attempts to repair growing divisions in the church's Western tradition. Emperor Charles V summoned the German estates of the Holy Roman Empire to a diet, a formal assembly, at Augsburg in Bavaria. He wanted to resolve the differences in a peaceful manner, particularly to solidify financial and military support for battles against Islamic forces that threatened the empire's borders.

The final version of the Augsburg Confession of 1530 was based on earlier tracts by Martin Luther and other evangelical statements of principle. Philip Melanchthon, a lay person, theologian, and teaching colleague of Luther, had the task of drafting the document itself. Once formulated, leaders of several estates signed the document. It was first read publicly on Saturday, June 25, 1530, at Augsburg.

The Augsburg Confession grounded what was taught in the Reformation on the foundation of Scripture and the tradition of the church. Although not offering a complete system of doctrine, the Augsburg Confession sets forth the primary teachings of our Lutheran heritage.

The Augsburg Confession became the chief document in a later collection of the crucial documents of the Lutheran Reformation. The collection was called the *Book of Concord* and was published on June 25, 1580, the 50th anniversary of the Augsburg Confession.

Besides the three ecumenical creeds and the Augsburg Confession, the *Book of Concord* included Luther's Small and Large Catechisms, the Apology to (that is, an elaboration on) the Augsburg Confession, Smalcald Articles, Formula of Concord, and other documents.

These writings are embraced not only by the Evangelical Lutheran Church in America. We share affirmation of the Augsburg Confession and the other writings in the *Book of Concord* with the whole communion of evangelical Lutheran churches throughout the world.

4

Church as Congregation

FOR LIFE AND WORK

When you or I tell someone, "We're going to church," we most likely are referring to worship in our congregations. The word *church* for most of us brings immediately to mind our own congregations. That is obvious and understandable.

Within our congregations, we mark many of the moments of greatest joy in life. We also are surrounded and upheld in times of deepest sorrow. We bring our children for Holy Baptism. We celebrate first communion and Confirmation (Affirmation of Baptism). We witness the joy of marriage. When death strikes a loved one, we are supported by prayer and the confession of faith by others, even when sorrow and tears may choke our own voices. And so, within our congregations, others may speak for us on such occasions; others lift their voices in faith and praise to God, reflecting the assurance of resurrection through Jesus Christ our Lord. Without hesitation, they—and we—confess:

> I believe in . . . the holy catholic Church,
> the communion of saints, the forgiveness of sins,
> the resurrection of the body, and the life everlasting.

With the power of music, we sing and ponder:

> *When we on that final journey go*
> *That Christ is for us preparing,*
> *We'll gather in song, our hearts aglow,*
> *All joy of the heavens sharing,*
> *And walk in the light of God's own place,*
> *With angels his name adoring.*[1]

Yes, church to us most often means our own congregation. After all, it is within our congregation that we witness most regularly what creates and establishes the church. As we recall from Article VII of the Augsburg Confession, we recognize the church as "the assembly of all believers among whom the Gospel is preached in its purity and the holy sacraments are administered according to the Gospel."[2] Within our congregation, we hear God's Word preached and taught. Within our congregation, we witness most regularly the sacrament of Holy Baptism. Within our own congregation, we share often in the sacrament of Holy Communion.

WHAT IS A CONGREGATION?

No wonder, then, the word *church* means most vividly for us our congregations. The central or key marks of "church" touch us most personally in our congregations. This awareness is reflected in the definition of a congregation within the Evangelical Lutheran Church in America: "A congregation is a community of baptized persons whose existence depends on the proclamation of the Gospel and the administration of the sacraments and whose purpose is to worship God, to nurture its members, and to reach out in witness and service to the world. To this end it assembles regularly for worship and nurture, organizes and carries out ministry to its people and neighborhood, and cooperates with and supports the wider church to strive for the fulfillment of God's mission in the world."[3]

The chief responsibilities of each congregation, according to this definition, are to:

1. Worship God
2. Nurture members in the faith
3. Reach out in witness and service
4. Minister within the immediate community
5. Participate with the wider church in God's mission in the world

This definition of a congregation echoes the Statement of Purpose of all three primary "expressions" of the Evangelical Lutheran Church in America—namely, congregations, synods, and churchwide ministries. All members of the ELCA are summoned to worship God, proclaim God's saving gospel, carry out Christ's Great Commission, serve in response to God's love in meeting human needs, nurture members in the Word of God, and manifest our unity in Christ (see pages 98-99 for the full text of our church's Statement of Purpose).

Perhaps a backyard barbecue grill provides a vivid illustration of the importance of active participation in our congregations. It also may show the significance of our congregations' connections with our synods and our whole church. Look at the barbecue coals that are the hottest ("liveliest," so to speak, and most effective). The coals that glow with the greatest heat are the ones closest to others. If a coal becomes separated from the rest and sits off by itself away from the heat and strength of the "community" of coals, it will not be effective by itself. Its heat may languish and even die. As a lukewarm coal, its potential for imparting its warmth is greatly diminished.

Awareness of the importance of our life together is aptly reflected in a statement of the Lutheran World Federation: "Each local church gathered around the preaching of the Gospel and the celebration of the sacraments is a realization of the universal church. . . . Through Word and sacraments every local church is bound into the wider communion of churches."[4]

In the hundreds of congregations that I have visited over the years, I have come to recognize certain signs of vitality in a congregation. The first is how seriously a congregation looks upon its own worship life and ministry within its community. The second is how deeply aware and committed a congregation is to ministry and mission through the wider church. Frankly, I have found no truly healthy congregation that was turned in upon itself or that cared only about its own interests and desires. Members in lively, spiritually vital congregations have allowed the gospel to lift their vision and open their hearts. They seem delighted by the mission God has given to us in our time.

WHAT DOES A CONGREGATION DO?

This sense of relationship, partnership, and commitment to the wider community of faith is reflected in the basic criteria for recognition of ELCA congregations. To be received and maintained as a congregation of the ELCA, a congregation by its "practice" as well as in its "governing documents" must pledge to:

1. preach the Word, administer the sacraments, and carry out God's mission;
2. accept this church's Confession of Faith;
3. agree to the Statement of Purpose of this church;
4. agree to call pastoral leadership from the clergy roster of this church . . . ;
5. agree to be responsible for its life as a Christian community; and
6. agree to support the life and work of this church [meaning the whole Evangelical Lutheran Church in America].[5]

Further, a congregation of the Evangelical Lutheran Church in America pledges, according to this church's constitution, to:

1. provide services of worship at which the Word of God is preached and the sacraments are administered;
2. provide pastoral care and assist all members to participate in this ministry [of the congregation];
3. challenge, equip, and support all members in carrying out their calling in their daily life and in their congregation;
4. teach the Word of God;
5. witness to the reconciling Word of God in Christ, reaching out to all people;
6. respond to human need, work for justice and peace, care for the sick and the suffering, and participate responsibly in society;
7. motivate its members to provide financial support for the congregation's ministry and the ministry of the synod and the churchwide organization;
8. foster and participate in interdependent relationships with other congregations, the synod, and the churchwide organization; [and]
9. foster and participate in ecumenical relationships consistent with churchwide policy.[6]

The center of life for each congregation is the Word of God— the Word as proclaimed and taught, the Word at work in the bath of rebirth (Baptism), and the Word as experienced in the meal of

Christ's presence (Holy Communion). Through the Word, God's people are sent forth to practice their faith in daily life. They also are called to serve in concert with other believers in the mission that God has given to the church in every age.

WHO ARE THE MEMBERS?

Four categories of membership are defined in the Model Constitution for Congregations of the Evangelical Lutheran Church in America. Here are those categories as expressed in the constitution for congregations:

1. *Baptized members* are those persons who have been received by the Sacrament of Holy Baptism in this congregation, or, having been previously baptized in the name of the Triune God, have been received by certificate of transfer from other Lutheran congregations or by affirmation of faith.
2. *Confirmed members* are baptized persons who have been confirmed in this congregation, those who have been received by adult baptism or by transfer as confirmed members from other Lutheran congregations, or baptized persons received by affirmation of faith.
3. *Voting members* are confirmed members. Such confirmed members shall have communed and made a contribution of record during the current or preceding year.
4. *Associate members* are persons holding membership in other Lutheran congregations who wish to retain such membership but desire to participate in the life and mission of this congregation. They have all the privileges and duties of membership except voting rights and eligibility for elected officers or membership on the Congregation Council . . . [since they possess such eligibility in the congregation in which they hold regular voting membership].[7]

The privilege and duty of members of each congregation are to:

1. make regular use of the means of grace, both Word and sacraments;
2. live a Christian life in accordance with the Word of God and the teachings of the Lutheran church; and

3. support the work of this congregation, synod, and the churchwide organization of the Evangelical Lutheran Church in America through contributions of their time, abilities, and financial support as biblical stewards.[8]

MANY SHAPES AND SIZES

Congregations exist in many shapes and sizes. For example, I grew up in a very small, rural congregation in North Dakota. In the years since my childhood, I have belonged to some other small or medium-sized congregations and to some very large ones as well.

In recent years, the average number of baptized members per congregation in the ELCA has been about 475. The average confirmed membership has been about 350.[9] While those numbers may reflect the average, they do not tell the whole story.

One-fourth of ELCA congregations (some 2,800) have 175 or fewer baptized members. Those congregations account for about six percent (300,000 in round figures) of all ELCA baptized members. By contrast, nearly 20 percent of ELCA members (about one million) are members of the nearly 450 ELCA congregations (four percent) with 1,501 or more members each. The largest ELCA congregation, Mount Olivet Lutheran Church in Minneapolis, has 13,000 members.

In between the smallest and largest congregations, we find nearly half (2.4 million) of ELCA members in the one quarter of ELCA congregations that have 501 to 1,500 members each. About 15 percent of ELCA members (nearly 700,000) are a part of the some 1,600 congregations (15 percent) with 351 to 500 members each. Another 15 percent of ELCA members are found in about 3,000 congregations (one-fourth of the total) that have 176 to 350 members each.

Half of ELCA congregations are in rural areas or small towns (that is, communities with a population of less than 10,000). Fifteen percent of ELCA congregations are linked directly to at least one other congregation in a parish arrangement.

Overall membership has remained fairly stable for U.S. Lutherans since 1970, although in recent years significant decreases have occurred.

The average number at worship in an ELCA congregation is 145, or about 30 percent of the ELCA's baptized membership, per

Sunday. By comparison, it can be noted that the average worship attendance in the Presbyterian Church (U.S.A.) is 45 percent of total membership and in the Assemblies of God, about 65 percent. Lutherans need renewed attention to regular participation in worship.

Lutheran women are more likely than men to participate regularly in worship. The most frequent participants are women over the age of 65, followed by those between ages 50 and 64. Men between 30 and 49 are the least likely to worship regularly. Twenty percent of ELCA members between 18 and 29 worship weekly compared with 46 percent of those 65 and over.

WITH $2 BILLION

The combined annual income of all ELCA congregations in the mid-1990s was about $2.7 billion. Most of those dollars were received in regular offerings. Some of it came through bequests and interest on investments. Beyond annual income, ELCA congregations reported having $1.8 billion in endowments, memorial funds, and savings. About two-thirds of ELCA congregations are without debt.

Congregation income, on average in the 1990s, grew at a rate greater than inflation. Of total income for ELCA congregations, nearly ten percent—on an overall average—is devoted to support of synodical and churchwide ministries. The rest is used for the average congregation's operating expenses, building improvements, debt payments, and other local needs.

Money devoted by congregations to the wider ministry of the church amounted to 18 percent in 1965; the percentage has declined steadily since then. At the same time, the amount of offering income devoted to a congregation's salaries and programs grew from 70 percent in 1970 to more than 80 percent in 1995.

AND HOW MANY MEMBERS?

In areas of declining population, some congregations have experienced a loss of members. A more significant factor in trends, however, has been the age of members. The median age of an ELCA member is about 50; that compares with a median age of 33 in the general U.S. population. So we are older than the general population. In terms of percentage of total membership, twice as many members of ELCA congregations, proportionately, are over age 75 than is the case in the general population.

About one-third of ELCA congregations report growth in membership. Another third are stable, and the remaining third indicate decline. Many growing congregations make follow-up contact with visitors at worship on the same day as their visit.

Members of ELCA congregations mirror the education levels of the general population. This means, according to surveys, just over half of ELCA members have a high school diploma or less. About one-fourth have attended college and another 15 percent have a college degree. Nearly ten percent have had graduate courses or have completed a graduate degree.

About 37 percent of the members of ELCA congregations identify themselves as Republican in party affiliation; 33 percent say they are independents; and 30 percent are Democrats.

A category in which ELCA members do not reflect the general population is in ethnic identity. Almost 98 percent of ELCA members are Caucasian. About one percent identify themselves as Black or African American; one-half percent as Hispanic or Latino; one-half percent as Asian; and just over one-tenth of one percent as American Indian or Alaska Native people.

RESPONSIBLE FOR INTERNAL LIFE

Normally, each ELCA congregation is incorporated. As a corporate entity a congregation is responsible for overseeing its internal life and operation.

Under a congregation's constitution, authority for governance resides in a legally called congregation meeting or assembly. Certain powers and responsibilities are delegated to the Congregation Council, a governing body elected by members of the congregation. (Congregation Council is the recommended name for the governing body, which has parallels in the other expressions of this church—namely, Synod Council in each synod and Church Council in the churchwide organization). In some congregations, the council is known as the board of administration, board of directors, or some other title.

Depending on a congregation's own constitution, the congregation's pastor may serve as *ex officio* president of the congregation or a lay member of the congregation may be elected as president. The duties of congregation officers and of the Congregation Council are to be stated in each congregation's constitution.

Authority to call the congregation's pastor resides within the congregation. As an ELCA congregation, however, the congregation has agreed to call only an ordained minister on the roster of the ELCA or a candidate approved for the roster, in accord with churchwide policy.

STRATEGIC ROLE OF A PASTOR

The calling of a pastor is one of the points where the life of the congregation intersects and interrelates directly with the responsibilities of the synod. Such a step in a congregation's life underscores the partnership of the congregation and synod. The unity of this whole church also is reflected in that decision in view of the fact that ELCA ordained ministers are listed on the roster of this whole church.

The gathering of a congregation through Word and Sacrament is not a matter of happenstance but rather of good order—order that specifically is related to ordained ministry within the life of the faith community. As stated in the churchwide constitution regarding ordained ministry, "Within the people of God and for the sake of the Gospel ministry entrusted to all believers, God has instituted the office of ministry of Word and Sacrament. To carry out this ministry, this church calls and ordains qualified persons."[10]

Ordained ministers of the ELCA are to be persons "whose commitment to Christ, soundness in the faith, aptness to preach, teach, and witness, and educational qualifications have been examined and approved in the manner prescribed in the documents of this church. . . ." Such pastors are to be "properly called and ordained." They must accept and adhere to the Confession of Faith of this church, be "diligent and faithful in the exercise of the ministry," lead a life that is "worthy of Gospel," and comply with the constitution of the Evangelical Lutheran Church in America.[11]

MINISTRY WITHIN LARGER CONTEXT

These standards and principles for ordained ministry in this church reflect our Lutheran heritage. As declared in the Augsburg Confession, "It is taught among us that nobody should publicly teach or preach or administer the sacraments in the church without a regular call."[12] Thus, those in ordained ministry are called to serve a specific role in a congregation or other setting within the larger ministry of the whole church.

As Philip Hefner of the Lutheran School of Theology at Chicago has written regarding ordained ministry, the specific role of pastors is "to ensure that the church does not forget who it is and what its purpose is." Dr. Hefner continued:

> The ordained ministry exists for the purpose of reminding the church in an explicit manner of its nature, goals, and mission. This involves the ordained ministry, first, in teaching, preaching, and presiding over sacramental life; second, in maintenance and governance; and third, in the actual work of caring for people within the church *(Seelesorge)* and strengthening them in faith and body so that they can share in the church's ministry.[13]

The "soul-care" of members within the congregation includes both nurture in the faith and a summons to witness and service. Herbert F. Brokering, a Lutheran pastor, has portrayed the purpose of such "soul-care" through a parable. He wrote:

> Once there was a church where the people took the offering back home with them. First it was collected and brought to the altar. After they asked God to bless it, they took it and put it back into their pockets. They mixed it up with all their other money, so that they couldn't tell which was blessed and which was not. Then they left. All week they spent as though each piece was blessed and was to be used lovingly.[14]

Within the Lutheran understanding of the faith, being a parent or spouse, a teacher or a clerk, a medical doctor or a laborer, or whatever one does in life is seen as doing God's work. We are nurtured in the faith within our congregations so that we can be good stewards of all that we have and do. As we pray in the offertory prayer:

Blessed are you, O Lord our God, maker of all things. Through your goodness you have blessed us with these gifts. With them we offer ourselves to your service and dedicate our lives to the care and redemption of all that you have made. . . .[15]

As sisters and brothers in Christ, we hear echoing in our midst that exhortation originally given to the congregation at Ephesus: "I . . . beg you to lead a life worthy of the calling to which you have been called, with all humility and gentleness, with patience, bearing with one another in love, making every effort to maintain the unity of the Spirit in the bond of peace. There is one body and one Spirit, just as you were called to the one hope of your calling, one Lord, one faith, one baptism. . . . So then, putting away falsehood, let all of us speak the truth to our neighbors, for we are members of one another . . . , and be kind to one another, tenderhearted, forgiving one another, as God in Christ has forgiven you" (Ephesians 4:1-5, 25, and 32).

Yes, we know "church" most closely in our own congregations. Within our congregations, we assemble for worship. Within our congregations, we are nourished in the faith. Within our congregations, we are strengthened for witness and service in daily life. And through our congregations, we join our hands with others in mission. In so doing, we discover the other two primary "expressions" of our church—the synod and churchwide organization.

5

Church as a Congregation
of Congregations

FOCUS ON WIDE TERRITORY

Perhaps we might describe a synod as a congregation of congregations. That description will not satisfy every theologian and lawyer. Some of them may prefer more technical language. But to speak of a congregation of congregations does give us some picture of being gathered together for the shared work of the church in a given territory.

All congregations of the Evangelical Lutheran Church in America (ELCA) are organized into 65 synods (meaning territories or jurisdictions). One of the 65 synods is non-geographical (the Slovak Zion Synod); all of the other 64 synods cover a specific geographical territory, some very compact and others large in square miles, depending on the number of members and congregations in a given area.

The average number of congregations in a synod is 170, although we will see that some synods are much larger or much smaller than average.

In fact, a great deal of variety is evident among the ELCA's synods. The largest in terms of baptized members, for example, is the Minneapolis Area Synod (about 228,000 in 175 congregations); yet it is the smallest geographically, covering only the city of Minneapolis and immediate suburbs.

Among the largest ELCA synods in the number of congregations per synod are the Northeastern Pennsylvania Synod (some 295 congregations and 167,000 members), the Northwestern Minnesota Synod (285 congregations and 112,800 members), and the

Southwestern Minnesota Synod (280 congregations and 139,000 members).

One of the smallest ELCA synods in terms of members (about 10,600) and congregations (some 30) is the Alaska Synod; yet it is the largest geographically, encompassing the whole state of Alaska (570,000 square miles, more than twice the size of the state of Texas). The Caribbean Synod is the smallest synod (about 6,500 members and three dozen congregations); its territory is divided by the waters of the Caribbean Sea and includes the commonwealth of Puerto Rico and the U.S. Virgin Islands.

For certain tasks and projects, the 65 synods of the ELCA are grouped in nine regions. The activities of these regions vary greatly, depending on what functions synods in a given region have chosen to assign to the region. Some regions have only a part-time staff person for coordination; that individual also may carry out other responsibilities in a given area on behalf of the churchwide organization.

"A WAY TOGETHER"

The word *synod* comes from two Greek words that mean "a way together." Congregations in a synod function together both through the synodical assembly and through the ongoing operation that is led by the synodical bishop and guided by the elected Synod Council. Just as a congregation has a Congregation Council, so the synod has a Synod Council. The council generally includes about 20 persons elected by the Synod Assembly, plus the synod's four officers—bishop, secretary, treasurer, and vice president (who serves as council chair).

The purpose of each synod is defined in the ELCA's churchwide constitution in this way: "Each synod, in partnership with the churchwide organization, shall bear primary responsibility for the oversight of the life and mission of this church in its territory."[1]

Our "way together" in the synod is reflected even in the vocabulary of our church. For example, we do not speak of "delegates" going from our congregations to a synod "convention." Instead, "voting members" gather in the synodical "assembly."

Actually, the terminology related to the legislative process of our church is no accident. The words *Synod Assembly* for the synod and *Churchwide Assembly* for the churchwide organization were deliberately chosen. These words reflect our churchly understanding of the three primary expressions of the Evangelical Lutheran Church in America, namely, as we have seen, congregations, synods, and churchwide organization. These "expressions" exist and serve within this one church.

For the Synod Assembly, people of the Evangelical Lutheran Church in America in each of the 65 synods are not sent as "delegates" or "messengers" from a given caucus or even congregation. Rather, they *assemble* as *members* of this church who have been selected for *voting* responsibilities for decisions and elections on behalf of the synod. The Synod Assembly is just that—an assembly of the people of this church, some of whom have been granted the responsibility of being *voting members* of the *Synod Assembly*. While the term *voting member* also has a technical meaning under certain state laws, it underscores for us our sense of participation as members in the life of this whole church.

In addition to the lay members chosen by congregations to serve as voting members, ordained ministers and other rostered persons under call also have voting privileges in the Synod Assembly.

Because we understand that our "congregations find their fulfillment in the universal community of the church [that is, the one holy apostolic church], and the universal church exists in and through congregations," we embrace the significance of being voting members in a given assembly. After all, as we declare in our church's governing documents regarding the Nature of the Church, the Evangelical Lutheran Church in America "derives its character and powers both from the sanction and representation of its congregations and from its inherent nature as an expression of the broader fellowship of the faithful."[2] We shall see in the next chapter the importance of this understanding in relation to the churchwide organization.

FROM THE EARLY DAYS

The gathering that we now call a synodical assembly is not new for Lutherans in North America. What became the first "synod" in North America was organized in Philadelphia in August 1748.

That "synod" came to be called the Ministerium of Pennsylvania and Adjacent States. In its early stages, its chief purpose focused on the placement of properly qualified and ordained pastors in the scattered Lutheran congregations of colonial times. Lutheran congregations were desperate for pastors. Opportunists would come around claiming to be pastors and congregations would call them. To guard against heresy and to protect congregations from imposters, several pastors and members of congregations met to form a synod.

That first synod—functioning primarily as a ministerium, that is, a gathering of pastors—met annually for seven years. Then, surprisingly, it ceased to function for five years after 1755. When it was reorganized in October 1760, the assembled participants discussed "whether it is necessary and advantageous" to meet annually. The conclusion was yes. According to the writings of Henry Melchior Muhlenberg, who was chosen again at that meeting as ministerium president, they declared:

> It is necessary and advantageous for laborers of the one Master and one vineyard to learn to know each other, unite themselves in love ever more closely for their common purpose, discuss whatever can be of most benefit to the *ecclesia plantanda* [planting and establishing of the church] and can extend the Christian religion. Everyone . . . can contribute . . . to the common good. Thus one can encourage, exhort, or comfort another. . . . Unity of spirit and harmony among the ministers of one confession make a great impression on the minds of their auditors. . . . Moreover, the irregular vagabond preachers who are a disgrace to our religion will thereby be somewhat curbed in their extravagant liberty to wander about, and hostile parties will have less opportunity to slander. Otherwise the intended temple will become a Babel and an even larger opening will be given to Satan and his apostles. On such occasions young preachers can profit from the experience of their elders. . . . For these reasons the meetings are to be continued.[3]

Although the issues and actions of assemblies of synods in the ELCA differ from the primary concerns of the early Ministerium of Pennsylvania, the need remains for "laborers of the one Master and one vineyard to learn to know each other, unite themselves in love ever more closely for their common purpose, [and] discuss whatever can be of most benefit" for extending the ministry of our church. Therefore, almost all synods gather annually in assembly. A few follow a biennial schedule for the synod's legislative assembly and hold a gathering of congregations for worship, workshops, and other events in the alternate years.

KEY PURPOSES

The basic purposes of the synod mirror those of congregations and the churchwide organization: (1) proclaim God's saving gospel; (2) carry out Christ's Great Commission; (3) serve in response to God's love to meet human needs; (4) worship God; (5) nurture members; and (6) manifest the unity of the body of Christ, the church. But the distinctive tasks of the synod in fulfilling these general purposes are defined in detail in the Constitution for Synods of the ELCA. Those tasks include: providing for pastoral care for the congregations, pastors, and other rostered leaders; planning for the work of this church within the territory of the synod; promoting interdependent relationships among the congregations, other synods, and the churchwide ministries; fostering support for shared ministries; building relationships with the educational institutions of this church; and encouraging organizations that focus especially on youth, women, and men. The actual list of responsibilities in the Constitution for Synods is a long one. That list is provided in the notes.[4]

STRATEGIC ROLE OF BISHOP

The list of duties of the synodical bishop is long, too, because the key figure in the fulfillment of the synod's responsibilities is the synodical bishop. The role of the bishop is one of oversight (that is, care, guidance, and leadership). The bishop is the synod's pastor. As the synod's pastor, the bishop is charged with responsibility to preach, teach, and administer the sacraments in accord with the faith of this church. Further, the bishop exercises this church's power to ordain, commission, or consecrate approved candidates. The synodical bishop also must provide leadership in the mission of this church. This includes: (1) interpreting the mission and theology of the whole church; (2) fostering support for and commitment to the mission of this church within this synod; and (3) coordinating the use of the resources available to the synod. We see this understanding underscored in great detail in the Constitution for Synods.[5]

SINCE THE REFORMATION

In a sense, Lutherans always have had bishops. At the time of the Lutheran Reformation in Germany, continuing use of the "episcopal" pattern in place in the Roman Catholic Church initially was assumed. Indeed, Lutheran flexibility in relation to church structure allowed the reformers to be willing to embrace those established forms, provided such leaders served the gospel. As stated in the Apology to the Augsburg Confession in Article XXVIII on "ecclesiastical power":

> We like the old division of power into the power of the order and the power of jurisdiction. Therefore, a bishop has the power of the order, namely, the ministry of Word and sacraments. He also has the power of jurisdiction, namely, the authority to excommunicate those who are guilty of public offenses or to absolve them, if they are converted and ask for absolution. A bishop does not have the power of a tyrant to act without a definite law, nor that of a king to act above the law. But he has a definite command, a definite Word of God, which he ought to teach and according to which he ought to exercise his jurisdiction.[6]

As stated in Article XXVIII of the Augsburg Confession, "bishops and pastors may make regulations so that everything in the churches is done in good order, but not as a means of obtaining God's grace or making satisfaction for sins. . . . It is proper for the Christian assembly to keep such ordinances for the sake of love and peace, to be obedient to the bishops and parish ministers in such matters, and to observe the regulations in such a way that one does not give offense to another and so that there may be no disorder or unbecoming conduct in the church."[7]

When keeping existing structures with bishops proved impossible in Germany, "superintendents" eventually were appointed to carry out the responsibility of oversight. Throughout the

Scandinavian countries, however, the office of bishop was retained in the years following the Lutheran Reformation there.

In North America, Lutheran immigrants suddenly found themselves in a new situation. The power of the state-church system that they had known in Europe no longer existed. Therefore, they had to find new forms to serve the needs of members and congregations. Those needs included efforts to provide pastors, to find means of theological education of future pastors and offer formal approval for the ordination of such candidates, to lead in the resolution of congregational conflicts, and, later, to join together in other education efforts and social ministry.

PRACTICE OF "OVERSIGHT"

For the function of regional "oversight," the term generally employed in North America until recently was *president*—that is, "synodical president" or "district president." Although called "presidents," they carried out the same responsibilities as Lutheran bishops elsewhere in the world. In so doing, their work reflected the duties of bishops within the general pattern of the whole church. It was not until 1970 in the ELCA's predecessor church body, The American Lutheran Church, that the name of the office began to change from *president* to *bishop*. That change in title was made in the predecessor Lutheran Church in America in 1980. Likewise, the Association of Evangelical Lutheran Churches used the term *bishop* for such officers. When the ELCA was formed, the pattern was in place. Those in the role of "oversight" would be called bishops.

Synodical bishops, assisted by members of each bishop's staff, serve in a variety of relationships. They relate directly to the needs and concerns of congregations, especially as congregations seek pastors. Just as was the case in colonial times for Pastor (and President) Muhlenberg, likewise today, duties in conflict resolution receive attention.

In addition, as we can see in the listing of the synodical bishop's responsibilities, the bishop is the strategic link in the synod in relation to churchwide ministries. Bishops also carry particular responsibilities together through the Conference of Bishops of the ELCA.

Yes, synodical bishops carry heavy responsibilities. The expectations of that office are high. The listing of formal duties is long. Yet the most strategic task is one of care for the unity of this church. After all, first on the list of tasks is this one: The bishop is to "preach, teach, and administer the sacraments in accord with the Confession of Faith of this church." Through such leadership, a synod can be seen clearly as our "way together" in the work that we share through this "expression" of the Evangelical Lutheran Church in America.

6

In the Wider Church

LESSON IN PRAYER

A well-formed Prayer of the Church in worship is shaped like an hourglass. Just as an hourglass is wide at the top, narrow in the middle, and wide at the bottom, so can be the concerns reflected in the Prayer of the Church.

Look at the form in *Lutheran Book of Worship* (pages 52-53). We begin with thanks for God's love, for salvation in Christ, for the gift of God's Spirit in the whole church, for the means of grace, and for our eternal hope. The prayer begins with that wide perspective.

Then, we narrow the focus of our concern and ask God specifically for mercy upon the church, on those who carry particular responsibilities within the life of the church, and on the mission we have in the world ("Save and defend your whole Church. . . . Give your wisdom and heavenly grace to all pastors and to those who hold office in your Church. . . . Send the light of your truth into all the earth . . . "). We then give attention to the needs of our nation and our common life in society ("Take from us all hatred and prejudice, give us the spirit of love, and dispose our days in your peace . . . ").

We narrow further our focus to our schools, homes, and work ("Bless the schools. . . . Sanctify our homes. . . . Let your blessing rest upon the seedtime and harvest, the commerce and industry . . . "). Then, very specifically, even by name, we offer to God our concerns for those within our congregations in special need ("Comfort with the grace of your Holy Spirit . . . ").

Just as the hourglass widens at the bottom, so a well-formed Prayer of the Church expands the range of concern as we remember all those who have gone before us in the faith ("We remember with thanksgiving . . . ").

In a way, the Prayer of the Church can model our participation in the life of the whole church. Within the lives of our congregations, we give immediate attention to preaching and teaching, sacramental ministry, education, witness, and service. We reflect care for the community around us.

Through our congregations we also join hands with others. Our "wider" ministry is carried out through our individual congregations in being part of a congregation of congregations—a synod. Still "wider" in range is the work that we do together through the churchwide ministries of the Evangelical Lutheran Church in America.

As we have seen, we as members of the Evangelical Lutheran Church in America have made a commitment: "This church shall seek to function as people of God through congregations, synods, and the churchwide organization, all of which shall be interdependent." Further, we understand that: "Each part, while fully the church, recognizes that it is not the whole church and therefore lives in a partnership relationship with the others."[1]

In a way, we might wish there were a simpler term to describe the churchwide work that we share. Some of us use phrases such as "wider church" or "greater church" in our conversations. The word *greater* carries some risk, especially if we mistakenly begin thinking that churchwide ministries are more important than those of each congregation or each synod. "Greater" must be understood as simply covering a larger area. "National church" once was used as a synonym for churchwide ministries. In recognition, however, that the territory of the Evangelical Lutheran Church in America extends beyond the borders of the United States of America, "national church" has not been employed in the ELCA.

In the governing documents, responsibility for the ELCA's churchwide ministries is assigned to the "churchwide organization." As we shall see, the range of that work is both wide—that is, global in scope—and yet specific, related to and supportive of our own congregations.

WORK OF CHURCHWIDE MINISTRIES

The role of the third "expression" of the ELCA, namely, the churchwide organization, is defined in this way:

> The Evangelical Lutheran Church in America shall have a churchwide organization that shall function interdependently with the congregations and synods of this church. The churchwide organization shall serve on behalf of and in support of this church's members, congregations, and synods in proclaiming the Gospel, reaching out in witness and service both globally and throughout the territory of this church, nurturing the members of this church in the daily life of faith, and manifesting the unity of this church with the whole Church of Jesus Christ.[2]

Key roles of the churchwide organization, as shown here, are to:

1. "function interdependently with the congregations and synods"; and
2. "serve on behalf of and in support of this church's members, congregations, and synods. . . ."

Echoing the Statement of Purpose[3] for all "expressions" of the ELCA, the efforts carried out through the churchwide organization are to focus on:

1. proclaiming the gospel;
2. reaching out in witness and service both globally and throughout the territory of this church;
3. nurturing the members of this church in the daily life of faith; and
4. manifesting the unity of this church with the whole church of Jesus Christ.

A further description of the work of the "wider" church, as we sometimes describe the churchwide organization, is provided in the churchwide constitution:

> The churchwide organization shall be an instrument for accomplishing the purposes of this church . . . that are shared with and supported by the members, congregations, and synods of this church. In keeping with this church's purposes, it shall develop churchwide policy, set standards for leadership, establish criteria for this church's endeavors, and coordinate the work of this

church. It shall be a means for the sharing of resources throughout this church, and shall provide programs and services as
determined by this church.[4]

The general purposes of the whole Evangelical Lutheran
Church in America give focus to churchwide ministries. Those are
carried out on behalf of and in support of the members, congregations, and synods of this church. Those purposes are outlined in
detail in the churchwide constitution.[5] Under those general purposes that shape all expressions of this church, numerous functions are to be fulfilled through the churchwide organization.[6] We
will see now how priorities and programs are shaped in churchwide ministries.

ASSEMBLY AND COUNCIL

The highest decision-making authority for this church is the
biennial Churchwide Assembly. Approximately 1,070 persons
are elected by the assemblies of the 65 synods to serve as voting
members of the Churchwide Assembly. Within the assembly, 60
percent of the voting members are laypersons (half of whom are
women and half of whom are men). The remaining voting members are clergy. Ten percent of the membership of the assembly
are to be persons of color or persons whose primary language is
other than English, according to the representation principles that
govern such assemblies.[7]

Between meetings of the Churchwide Assembly, the Church
Council exercises "interim legislative authority" and serves as the
board of directors for the churchwide organization.[8] The 33 members of the Church Council are elected by the Churchwide Assembly. The council also includes the four churchwide officers—the
presiding bishop, secretary, and treasurer, who serve as full-time,
salaried officers, and the vice president, who is non-salaried and
serves as chair of the Church Council.

In addition to the Church Council, the Churchwide Assembly
also elects the members of program committees, boards and particular committees, acts on statements and resolutions that define
policy in this church, and approves an expenditure plan.

The operation of the churchwide organization is further
defined in this way: "Leadership of this church shall be vested

in the officers, the Churchwide Assembly, the Church Council, boards, and executive directors of churchwide administrative units. . . ."[9] Further, we read:

> The churchwide organization shall carry out its duties through functional elements known as units. Units shall be responsible to the Churchwide Assembly and the Church Council in the interim between regular meetings of the assembly.[10]

Overseeing the overall operation of the churchwide organization is the bishop of this church. The presiding bishop works with others, especially the officers and executive directors of the churchwide units, in accomplishing the work assigned to the churchwide organization. Coordination is carried out through the Administrative Team, Cabinet of Executives, and other "tables" for collaboration. A bylaw describes the role of the Administrative Team in this way:

> The presiding bishop, secretary, treasurer, and executive for administration shall function as an administrative team, directed by the presiding bishop. This administrative team shall assist the presiding bishop in the fulfillment of the presiding bishop's responsibilities for oversight, management, supervision, and coordination in the operation of the churchwide organization.[11]

Seven program units are responsible for key areas of work on behalf of congregations through the ELCA's churchwide organization. They are:

1. Evangelical Outreach and Congregational Mission;
2. Global Mission;
3. Vocation and Education;
4. Church in Society;
5. Multicultural Ministries;
6. Publishing House of the ELCA; and
7. Women of the ELCA.

The primary tasks of each of these program units are:

1. Evangelical Outreach and Congregational Mission: "The Evangelical Outreach and Congregational Mission unit shall foster and facilitate the efforts of congregations, synods, and related institutions and agencies in reaching out in witness to the Gospel to people in all contexts and cultures within the territory of this church. It will do so by equipping existing congregations and ministries; developing new ministries and congregations; seeking to renew strategic ministries; and working with congregations and synods in programs and strategies for renewal and evangelical outreach."[12] For example,

♦ In the first two decades of the ELCA's life, about 513 new congregations were established through the support of what was first known as the Division for Outreach and now is identified as the Evangelical Outreach and Congregational Mission unit to underscore its primary focus.

♦ About 30 to 40 new ministries are begun each year, many of which eventually developed into established congregations.

♦ Special training is provided through this unit for pastors called to develop new ministries and congregations.

♦ About fifteen percent of the funds for churchwide ministries are allocated to starting new congregations and supporting rural and urban ministries in special need.

2. Global Mission: This unit is responsible for this church's mission in other countries and shall be the channel through which churches in other countries engage in mission to this church and society.[13] To do so, the unit (a) establishes relationships and cooperates in mission with Lutheran and other Christian churches, agencies, institutions, mission societies, and movements in other countries; (b) develops and recommends policies and programs for this church's mission in other countries; (c) provides contacts and the exchange of human and material resources among churches, institutions, and agencies outside the U.S.A. with which this unit cooperates; and (d) recruits, calls, and sends missionary personnel, including volunteers. The Global Mission unit also participates in development and relief with Lutheran World Relief, the Lutheran World Federation, and other ecumenical organizations and agencies. For example,

♦ About one-fourth of all funds for churchwide ministries is devoted to global mission and international hunger relief and development.

♦ Some 400 missionaries serve on behalf of the ELCA in partner Lutheran churches in 40 countries.

3. Vocation and Education: This unit is "responsible for development and support of faithful, wise, and courageous leaders whose vocations serve God's mission in the world" and is to "assist this church and its institutions in equipping people to practice their callings under the Gospel for the sake of the world." In so doing, the unit must "articulate and exemplify for this church a guiding vision that cultivates the Lutheran understanding of the vocation of all the baptized and the place of education and knowledge in the context of faith. . . ."[14] The unit also is responsible for the educational activities of this church through its colleges and universities, campus ministries, early childhood education centers, and elementary and secondary schools.[15] For example,

♦ Each year some 2,300 students attend the eight ELCA seminaries. Most of them are preparing for pastoral ministry.

♦ About 50,000 students are enrolled each year in the 28 ELCA-related colleges and universities.

♦ Lutheran campus ministry serves at about 150 public college and universities, maintaining contact and ministry with Lutheran students on those campuses. Over the decades, the Lutheran Student Association has been an important influence in the life of many people.

♦ The Lutheran Youth Organization is part of this unit, and the unit also relates to outdoor ministry programs.

♦ Funding for the ELCA seminaries is provided both through the churchwide organization and by each synod. Many congregations also provide tuition aid to seminary students from such congregations.

♦ Money from the ELCA for this church's colleges and universities is provided by grants through this unit and through funds given by members, congregations, and synods, in addition to tuition, fees, and others gifts and grants.

♦ About 2,500 congregations operate early childhood education centers, elementary schools, or secondary schools involving a quarter million students.

4. Church in Society: This unit is to "assist this church to discern, understand, and respond to the needs of human beings, communities, society, and the whole creation through direct human services and through addressing systems, structures, and policies of society, seeking to promote justice, peace, and the care of the earth. . . ."[16] The duties of this unit, therefore, include coordination of this church's theological and ethical study and analysis of social issues as part of its social witness. In addition, this unit develops social statements, is responsible for this church's efforts to combat hunger, relates on behalf of this church to Lutheran Immigration and Refugee Service and the Inter-Lutheran Domestic Disaster Response, and coordinates this church's domestic disaster response. For example,

♦ About 250 Lutheran social ministry organizations serve 1.8 million children and adults each year.

♦ A vast social service system is maintained throughout the United States by Lutherans. Within many states, strong Lutheran Social Services programs of counseling, foster care, adoption services, chemical-dependency treatment, low-income housing, and other programs are found. Further, a quarter of the nonprofit beds in nursing-care homes for the elderly in the United States are in Lutheran institutions.

♦ A Washington office for advocacy and the Lutheran Office for World Community at the United Nations are the responsibility of this unit.

5. Multicultural Ministries: This unit is to "guide the churchwide organization in the multicultural dimensions of its work." In so doing, the Multicultural Ministries unit is to "foster programs of the churchwide organization with synods, regions, and agencies and institutions as they identify, develop, and strengthen the multicultural dimensions of their work" and also "coordinate the churchwide implementation of ethnic-specific ministry strategies."[17]

6. Publishing House of the ELCA: The Publishing House of the ELCA, commonly known as Augsburg Fortress, Publishers, is responsible for the publishing ministry of this church.[18] Unlike the first five program units, which are supported through the churchwide budget, the ELCA publishing house must be self-sustaining through the sale of its published resources.

7. Women of the ELCA: The Women of the ELCA, as a churchwide program unit, is to assist women throughout this church "to commit themselves to full discipleship, affirm their gifts, and support each other in their particular callings."[19] In addition to regular meetings in congregations, synodical gatherings are held annually, and every three years, a churchwide gathering occurs. At the churchwide gathering, the members of the executive board of Women of the ELCA are elected to three-year terms.

CHURCHWIDE SERVICE UNITS

In addition to the program units, service units operate on behalf of and in support of congregations, synods, and churchwide ministries. They include:

1. Communication Services;
2. *The Lutheran* magazine;
3. Foundation of the ELCA;
4. Development Services;
5. Mission Investment Fund of the ELCA; and
6. Board of Pensions of the ELCA.

The Communication Services unit is to interpret the work of this church in a variety of ways and coordinate the communication activities of churchwide units.[20] Serving as a crucial link for communication is *The Lutheran* magazine, a key resource for members in fostering greater awareness of the vitality and scope of this church's witness and service throughout the U.S.A. and beyond.[21]

The Foundation of the ELCA provides opportunities for members to undertake major gifts and deferred giving programs, as well as investment services for endowment funds.[22] The Development Services unit coordinates the various efforts to foster financial support for church ministries and special endeavors, such as responses to national and international disasters.[23]

The Mission Investment Fund of the ELCA offers opportunities for individuals and congregations to invest funds that, in turn, are used to provide loans to new and existing congregations or organizations of this church. Through this means, for instance, a developing congregation may be able to afford to construct a worship center and other facilities for ministry.[24]

The Board of Pensions, through contributions and premiums, provides retiree benefits, as well as health, dental, and disability benefits to church workers.[25] A comprehensive program for such benefits is crucial for controlling costs and ensuring adequate coverage for individuals and families throughout active service and in retirement. The ELCA's pension program grows out of a tradition of Lutheran care for church workers that represented, in its beginning in the mid-1800s, one of the earliest pension plans in the U.S.A.

IN MISSION TOGETHER

Throughout the years, outstanding institutions have been created by Lutherans in North America. These institutions continue to serve as strategic arms or entities of this church for fulfilling our shared needs and for serving God's mission in the world. They are part of this church. They are "church," but not in the same sense as congregations, synods, and the churchwide organization. Yet, they help fulfill the mission that we believe God has given us on the threshold of a new century.

How are the institutional relationships of this church characterized in our governing documents?

Seminaries

Look first at seminaries. This church's seminaries are viewed as most intimately related to the life of this church. The recognized role of ordained ministry in the whole life of the church undergirds the special relationship with seminaries. As stated in the ELCA churchwide constitution: "This church shall sponsor, support, and provide for oversight of seminaries for the preparation of persons for the ordained and other ministries and for continuing study on the part of ordained ministers and laypersons."[26] Further, the churchwide bylaws indicate: "Each seminary shall be a seminary of this church, shall be incorporated, and shall be governed by its board of directors consistent with policies established by the Church Council."[27] Other bylaws underscore this understanding of each seminary being "a seminary of this church."

> In accordance with the governing documents of each seminary, the board of directors shall elect the president of the seminary in consultation with the presiding bishop of this church and the appropriate churchwide unit as designated by the Church Council, elect and retain faculty and administrative officers, and approve educational policies and programs for persons preparing for public ministry. . . .[28]

The ELCA seminaries receive both churchwide and synodical financial support.[29] In addition, financial needs of the seminaries are met through tuition, fees, endowment income, and fund-raising efforts.[30]

The Rev. Phyllis Anderson, when she served on the churchwide

staff with responsibilities related to theological education, underscored some important developments for the future of Lutheran
seminary education. Dr. Anderson explained, "Seminaries [of the
ELCA] are building a network that will include many partners." What
is being developed, she said, "will serve not only those who prepare
for pastoral ministry, but also a host of other ministries. . . . New
technologies and new approaches are making . . . Lutheran theological education flexible, accessible, and adaptable" to meet the needs of
present and future pastors, those on the official lay rosters, members
of congregations, and others.[31]

The emerging shape of the ELCA seminaries is grounded in a
major study of theological education in the early 1990s. As a result
of that study, significant steps were approved by the 1993 and 1995
Churchwide Assemblies. Decisions were made on how we as a church
will prepare the leaders whom we need for a changing mission situation, how we will financially support theological education, and how
the relationships of this church and its seminaries will evolve.

Clearly, as Dr. Anderson said, theological education is needed
to maintain a strong Lutheran witness in an increasingly secular
society.

Colleges and Universities

Strategic institutions related to our church include the 28 colleges and universities of the Evangelical Lutheran Church in
America. In contrast to this church's seminaries, greater variety is
envisioned in the relationship of the congregations, synods, and
churchwide organization to the colleges and universities of this
church.[32] The principles that shape the relationship are described
in this way:

> The relationship of this church to its colleges and universities
> shall be guided by policies fostering educational institutions
> dedicated to the Lutheran tradition wherein such institutions
> are . . . [to be] faithful to the will of God as institutions pro-
> viding quality instruction in religion and a lively ministry of
> worship, outreach, and service; diligent in their preparation
> of leaders committed to truth, excellence, and ethical values;
> and pledged to the well-being of students in the development
> of mind, body, and spirit.[33]

Specific patterns of governance for the ELCA colleges and universities are defined in each institution's documents.[34] Often the pattern reflects in some way the particular history of a given institution. Further, such matters as representation of members of this church on the institution's board, limitation of terms for board members, whether the college or university president must be a member of this church, and representation of synodical bishops on a given board are determined by each institution.[35]

Compassion and Mercy

Through a solid, deeply felt Lutheran commitment to showing compassion and meeting human need, a Lutheran social ministry system began to emerge in the 1800s and has grown since then.

The relationship of the three primary expressions of this church—congregations, synods, and churchwide organization—to institutions and agencies is described in this way: "This church shall seek to meet human needs through encouragement of its people to individual and corporate action, and through establishing, developing, recognizing, and supporting institutions and agencies that minister to people in their spiritual and temporal needs."[36]

Responsibility for social ministry is assigned in the churchwide organization to the Church in Society unit (as cited above). Through that unit, criteria are developed for affiliation with this church of Lutheran Social Service agencies and other social ministry organizations.

An important development was the formation in 1996 of Lutheran Services in America. This inter-Lutheran organization was established as an alliance of Lutheran social ministries with the ELCA and The Lutheran Church–Missouri Synod. About 280 Lutheran social ministry organizations exist in the United States. They are of various sizes and reflect a diverse range of services. Trends in society and government underscore the need for partnership. Working together, Lutheran social ministries can continue to be one of the largest providers of human services in the nation.

Lutheran Services in America is to: (1) foster continued, conscientious responses by Lutheran social ministries to human need; (2) affirm the ongoing relationships of such ministries with congregations, synods, and the respective church bodies; and (3) underscore in society the concerns of the church for healing, justice, and wholeness.

Cooperative Efforts

Both Lutheran World Relief (LWR) and Lutheran Immigration and Refugee Service (LIRS) are cooperative efforts carried out jointly by the ELCA with The Lutheran Church–Missouri Synod. Lutheran World Relief was born in the closing days of World War II to provide relief assistance in the aftermath of that war. The need for such international relief and development persisted elsewhere in the world, even after the immediate post-war assistance had been provided. So Lutheran World Relief continued to serve as the relief-and-development arm of U. S. Lutherans. Now the work of LWR is supported by ELCA hunger appeal funds. Those funds also are shared with the Lutheran World Federation in a coordinated, global strategy of emergency relief and ongoing development.

Almost before you or I hear of some disaster or emergency situation elsewhere in the world, Lutherans are already there with assistance either directly through LWR and LWF world service or by means of ecumenical cooperation with other reputable agencies.

The need for refugee care continues unabated. Therefore, Lutheran Immigration and Refugee Service addresses such concerns on behalf of U.S. Lutherans. While the principal areas from which refugees come for resettlement change over the years, Lutherans assist through LIRS such refugees in their efforts to find a new home where they can live and work freely.

Inter-Lutheran Disaster Response represents a joint effort to provide emergency assistance in response to domestic disasters, be they hurricanes, earthquakes, floods, bombings, or other devastation. Lutherans move in with immediate help and also stay there for the long haul in response to continuing needs.

Ecumenical Relationships

In the wider arena, the ELCA is the second largest member church of the Lutheran World Federation (the Church of Sweden is the largest). The ELCA also is a member of the World Council of Churches and the National Council of the Churches of Christ in the U.S.A.

Major ecumenical developments transpired toward the end of the twentieth century. Many of those breakthroughs manifested reception of the results of decades of dialogue. On October 31, 1999, the *Joint Declaration on the Doctrine of Justification* was signed by representatives of the Lutheran World Federation and the Roman Catholic Church at Augsburg, Germany. Among the six Lutherans signing on behalf of the LWF was the Rev. H. George Anderson of the ELCA in his role as an LWF vice president.

The Evangelical Lutheran Church in America also entered into agreements of "full communion," or official mutual recognition, with several churches. These opened the door for official church-to-church cooperation in strategic ways. A relationship of "full communion" represents a mutual recognition of the churches and allows for the availability of service by ordained ministers upon invitation of the partner churches.

In 1997, the ELCA's Churchwide Assembly approved with three Reformed churches (Presbyterian Church [U.S.A.], Reformed Church in America, and United Church of Christ) the document, "A Formula of Agreement." Similar "full communion" relationships with the Moravian Church and The Episcopal Church were approved by the ELCA's 1999 Churchwide Assembly. The agreement with the Moravian Church was known as "Following our Shepherd to Full Communion." "Called to Common Mission" was the name of the ELCA-Episcopal agreement.

The purpose of these relationships of full communion is the opening of possibilities for common mission for the sake of the Gospel.

EMBRACING THE GLOBE

Our churchwide ministries—like those of each congregation, each synod, and the various institutions of this church—reveal that:

1. We Lutherans are a praying people. (Worship is at the center of our church life, for we understand that the church is created and sustained by Word and Sacrament.)
2. We Lutherans are a singing people. (A grand tradition of music emerged from and continues to reflect our Reformation heritage. Indeed, where would the world be without J. S. Bach and the vast throng of other Lutheran musicians who enable us to give praise to God with artistic beauty?)

3. We Lutherans are a learning people. (The Lutheran Reformation was born in a university and our emphasis on education continues both in our congregations and through our other ministries, including colleges, universities, seminaries, and other programs.)

4. We Lutherans are a serving people. (Consider the crucial ministries of compassion, mercy, social service, emergency relief, and development that have been created and continued by the Lutheran church with the support that you and I provide.)

Through the ELCA churchwide ministries, you and I—and all the other members of the 10,500 ELCA congregations—embrace the needs of the world. We respond through witness and service in the name of Jesus. We do so as we join hands with others for international and domestic outreach for the sake of the gospel. We also do so through ministries of care, relief, compassion, mercy, and hope.

As we undertake together our ELCA's churchwide ministries, we give hands and feet, body and heart to our confession, "We believe in one holy catholic and apostolic Church. . . ."

7

United for a Common Purpose

CHURCH AS BODY

The apostle Paul offered a vivid portrait of the church. He characterized the church as the body of Christ in the world. As he wrote to the congregation at Corinth, so the description holds true for us, even in this third millennium of Christian witness:

> For just as the body is one and has many members, and all the members of the body, though many, are one body, so it is with Christ. . . . Indeed, the body does not consist of one member but of many. If the foot would say, "Because I am not a hand, I do not belong to the body," that would not make it any less a part of the body. And if the ear would say, "Because I am not an eye, I do not belong to the body," that would not make it any less a part of the body. If the whole body were an eye, where would the hearing be? If the whole body were hearing, where would the sense of smell be? But as it is, God arranged the members in the body, each one of them, as he chose. . . . As it is, there are many members, yet one body. . . . Now you are the body of Christ and individually members of it (1 Corinthians 12:12ff).

Later the apostle Paul goes on to speak of the need for good order in the life of the church. He explores how the body of Christ is to be organized for the well-being of all members.

Yes, the church—what a body, what a marvelous body created by Word and Sacrament and sent forth in mission. The church—what a body, indeed! The church, united and working for a common, shared purpose—the mission that God has given in our time. Indeed, we are summoned as one great cloud of witnesses.

DIVINELY CREATED, HUMANLY ORGANIZED

As a result, we Lutherans point to the church both as a mystical or spiritual reality and as a human organization. Indeed, the church is created by God at work through the proclamation of the gospel and the administration of the sacraments. As we see in Article VII of the Augsburg Confession, "The church is the assembly of saints in which the Gospel is taught purely and the sacraments are administered rightly. . . ."[1]

The English word *church* is derived from the Greek *ekklesia,* which means "assembly," and *kyriake,* which means "belonging to the Lord." The most basic meaning of "church," therefore, is the worshiping assembly called into being and sent into ministry by God.[2]

As the reformers declared in the Apology to the Augsburg Confession, "We must understand what it is that chiefly makes us members, and living members, of the church. If we were to define the church as only an outward organization embracing both the good and the wicked, then . . . [folk] would not understand that the kingdom of Christ is the righteousness of the heart and the gift of the Holy Spirit. . . ."[3]

Further, however, the reformers pointed out, "We are not dreaming about some Platonic republic . . . , but we teach that this church actually exists. . . . In accordance with the Scriptures, therefore, we maintain that the church in the proper sense is the assembly of saints who truly believe the Gospel of Christ and who have the Holy Spirit."[4]

The Apology to the Augsburg Confession underscores the core of what constitutes the church in this way:

> The church is not merely an association of outward ties and rites like other civic governments, however, but it is mainly an association of faith and of the Holy Spirit in . . . [human] hearts. To make it recognizable, this association has outward marks, the pure teaching of the Gospel and the administration of the sacraments in harmony with the Gospel of Christ. This church alone is called the body of Christ, which Christ renews, consecrates, and governs by his Spirit. . . .[5]

In the Large Catechism, Luther spoke of God having, through the church, "a unique community in the world." To underscore

God's life-giving work through this unique community, Luther said of the church: "It is the mother that begets and bears every Christian through the Word of God. The Holy Spirit reveals and preaches that Word, and by it he illumines and kindles hearts so that they grasp and accept it, cling to it, and persevere in it."[6]

Indeed, as Gustaf Aulén, a distinguished church leader and twentieth-century theologian, wrote: "The church and Christ belong together. . . . The church exists in and through Christ. Where Christ is, there is the church. . . . Under the conditions of this earthly life the church is the mode of the living and active revelation of Christ."[7]

SPECIAL PATTERN OF ORGANIZATION

Lutherans do not claim that any particular pattern of church organization is biblically mandated. No church structure has been viewed either as God-given or absolute. In fact, the Lutheran emphasis on the gospel and sacraments as the center of the church's life has kept Lutherans free to employ a variety of church structures. Most of the common forms of church order are found in Lutheran churches throughout the world.

Some churches follow a heavily congregational pattern, in which congregations are seen as autonomous, sometimes even in determination of their own creeds and doctrine. Others may be viewed as more episcopal in church governance and operation— that is, with bishops, priests, and laity being given a strong role in the church body's life. Still others resemble a somewhat presbyterian style in which elected representatives within the congregation and within regional and general assemblies make decisions for a congregation or church body. Many reflect a mix of those patterns. Obviously, from such a variety of organizational styles, we can see Lutherans are pragmatic, rather than dogmatic, about church order. The ELCA might be characterized as having "congrepiscopresbyterial" governance and organization.

As Kent S. Knutson, a brilliant theologian who served as the president of The American Lutheran Church from 1971 until his untimely death in 1973, once wrote: "The Gospel can be served well by any number of structural arrangements. There can be no final or perfect structure. . . . While the Gospel and the basic mission of the Church do not change, the continuing changes in our society confront us with new opportunities, possibilities, and problems. We must be ready to adjust our structures from time to time because the situation into which God sends us changes and because through experience we may become wiser."[8]

Lutherans do understand, however, that church order and organization are important. After all, as the apostle Paul teaches about the life of the church, "All things should be done decently and in order" (1 Corinthians 14:40).

"EXTERNAL SCAFFOLDING"

Henry Melchior Muhlenberg spoke of the organizational structure of the church as "the external scaffolding of the spiritual edifice."[9] Muhlenberg, a giant among early Lutheran leaders in North America, sought an organizational pattern that would reflect and practice what the Augsburg Confession declares about the church as the assembly of believers gathered by Word and Sacrament.

As reflected throughout the world as well as in North America, the "external scaffolding" of Lutheran churches has been arranged in various ways. Many of these organizational structures were dictated by responses to particular needs; others were shaped in reaction to past experience.

Although no specific pattern for church organization is mandated biblically, the teaching of Scripture and the heritage of the Reformation shape the organization and operation of the whole Evangelical Lutheran Church in America.

Undergirding the ELCA's organization is a profound awareness of the apostle Paul's image of the church as the body of Christ. Thus, when defining both the whole church universal and the ELCA in particular, the ELCA's churchwide constitution declares:

> The Church [that is, the whole church of Jesus Christ] is a people created by God in Christ, empowered by the Holy Spirit, called and sent to bear witness to God's creative, redeeming, and sanctifying activity in the world.[10]

> This church [specifically the Evangelical Lutheran Church in America] shall seek to function as people of God through congregations, synods, and the churchwide organization, all of which

shall be interdependent. Each part, while fully the church, recognizes that it is not the whole church and therefore lives in a partnership relationship with the others.[11]

For the sake of understanding the significance of this provision, we need to ponder the key points:

1. Acknowledgment of and testimony to the whole church as created, called, and sent by God.
2. Acknowledgment of the unity of this church—namely, "This church shall seek to function as people of God."
   a. Note the definite article is missing; the ELCA does not claim to be "the," meaning exclusive of all others, "people of God."
   b. Rather, the people of the ELCA are to "seek to function as people of God" through the life of this church.
3. Acknowledgment of the ecclesial organizational elements (that is, the primary "expressions") of this church—namely, congregations, synods, and the churchwide organization.
4. Acknowledgment of the intimately interconnected and interrelated existence of these elements or ecclesial "expressions"—namely, through the declaration of their *inter*dependence, rather than independence.
   a. Each part is fully church.
   b. Each part, however, is not the whole church.
   c. Therefore, each part is summoned to partnership.

PARTNERSHIP FOR THREE "EXPRESSIONS"

In this definition of how we are to worship, witness, serve, and live together as a church, notions of hierarchy in structure are rejected. Instead, all three primary "expressions" of this church—namely, congregations, synods, and the churchwide organization—are understood as "fully the church," yet each is to serve in partnership with the others.

A deeper understanding of this partnership guards against chaos. Each primary expression has particular responsibilities. How we in the ELCA are to practice being "church" is explained under the Principles of Organization in the churchwide constitution:

The congregations, synods, and churchwide organization of this church are interdependent partners sharing responsibly in God's mission. In an interdependent relationship primary responsibility for particular functions will vary between the partners. . . .[12]

Using Muhlenberg's picturesque phrase, we can say that the "external scaffolding" of the Evangelical Lutheran Church in America reflects an awareness of both the crucial importance of each community of believers assembled by Word and Sacrament and of the whole church serving in God-given mission. At the same time, the churchly character of synodical and churchwide ministries is embraced.

Under the ecclesiology (that is, the theological understanding) and polity of the Evangelical Lutheran Church in America, the congregations, synods, and churchwide organization of this church are recognized as possessing an inherent ecclesial[13] (or churchly) character. This recognition undergirds the use of the word *expressions* in relation to the congregations, synods, and churchwide organization.

Congregations

The central, churchly work of congregations is summarized in the following constitutional provision: "The congregation shall include in its mission a life of worship and nurture for its members, and outreach in witness and service to its community."[14] Clearly, each congregation is the basic element in the life of the whole ELCA. After all, where most of us know "church" most regularly and closely is in our own congregations.

Yet as members of the ELCA, we recognize the "church" work that takes place beyond our own congregations. Indeed, that work is done on behalf of and in support of each of us in each congregation.

Synods

So we find that the churchly work of the synods is described in this way: "The synod shall provide for pastoral care of the congregations, ordained ministers, and associates in ministry, deaconesses, and diaconal ministers within its boundaries. It shall develop resources for the life and mission of its people and shall enlarge the ministries and extend the outreach into society on behalf of and in connection with the congregations and the churchwide organization."[15]

Churchwide Organization

Further, the churchly work of the churchwide organization is defined: "The churchwide organization shall implement the extended mission of the Church, developing churchwide policies in consultation with the synods and congregations, entering into relationship with governmental, ecumenical, and societal agencies in accordance with accepted resolutions and/or in response to specific agreed-upon areas of responsibility."[16]

The principle of interdependence or partnership reflects a biblical and theological understanding of the church and its work. To underscore the churchly use of the concept of interdependence, a contrast is drawn to the way that word might be used in other situations. As stated in the ELCA's governing documents:

> References herein to the nature of the relationship between the three primary expressions of this church—congregations, synods, and the churchwide organization—as being interdependent or as being in a partnership relationship describe the mutual responsibility of these expressions in God's mission, and the fulfillment of the purposes of this church as described in chapter 4, and do not imply or describe the creation of partnerships, co-ventures, agencies, or other legal relationships recognized in civil law.[17]

SHARED PURPOSE IN MISSION

All three primary expressions of the Evangelical Lutheran Church in America—and all of this church's institutions and related organizations—work for the sake of God's mission in the world. After all, we are part of one body:

> In faithful participation in the mission of God in and through this church, congregations, synods, and the churchwide organization—as interdependent expressions of this church—shall be guided by the biblical and confessional commitments of this church. Each shall recognize that mission efforts must be shaped by both local needs and global awareness, by both individual witness and corporate endeavor, and by both distinctly Lutheran emphases and growing ecumenical cooperation.[18]

Since congregations, synods, and the churchwide organization are partners that share in God's mission, all share in the responsibility to develop, implement, and strengthen the financial support program of this church.[19]

Although the three primary "expressions" of the ELCA have distinctive functions, all share a common purpose. Indeed, the same Statement of Purpose is found in chapter 4 of the Model Constitution for Congregations, chapter 6 of the Constitution for Synods, and chapter 4 of the churchwide constitution. As members of the ELCA, we are summoned together to:

1. Worship God
2. Proclaim God's saving gospel
3. Carry out Christ's Great Commission
4. Serve in response to God's love in meeting human needs
5. Nurture members in the Word of God for growth in faith
6. Manifest unity

Note, however, that all of these activities are part of a broader task—namely, participating in God's mission in the world. Indeed, as we read in the Model Constitution for Congregations:

To participate in God's mission, this congregation as part of the Church shall:

1. Worship God in proclamation of the Word and administration of the sacraments and through lives of prayer, praise, thanksgiving, witness, and service.
2. Proclaim God's saving Gospel of justification by grace for Christ's sake through faith alone, according to the apostolic witness in the Holy Scripture, preserving and transmitting the Gospel faithfully to future generations.
3. Carry out Christ's Great Commission by reaching out to all people to bring them to faith in Christ and by doing all ministry with a global awareness consistent with the understanding of God as Creator, Redeemer, and Sanctifier of all.
4. Serve in response to God's love to meet human needs, caring for the sick and the aged, advocating dignity and justice for all people, working for peace and reconciliation among the nations, and standing with the poor and powerless, and committing itself to their needs.

5. Nurture its members in the Word of God so as to grow in faith and hope and love, to see daily life as the primary setting for the exercise of their Christian calling, and to use the gifts of the Spirit for their life together and for their calling in the world.

6. Manifest the unity given to the people of God by living in the love of Christ and by joining with other Christians in prayer and action to express and preserve the unity which the Spirit gives.[20]

Together, we seek to fulfill these purposes. After all, as members of the Evangelical Lutheran Church in America, we are united for a common purpose.

8

What We Are and Do

FOR WIDE VISION

A profoundly important sense of the whole church was embraced, affirmed, and maintained in the Lutheran Reformation of the sixteenth century. Beyond the basic reforms that were sought in the life of the church at that time, Luther and his colleagues looked upon many aspects of church structure as they knew it. They did not set out to create a separate church. They remained in apostolic succession. That is, they continued to preach and teach the faith once delivered to the saints.

When the necessity of the times required the reformers to establish some church organization, they did so within their own context. As a result, for them, the ongoing intersection of church order and government power—what came to be known as the European state-church system—continued. They undertook pragmatic responses to urgent needs. Their steps included regional visits to congregations. They also prepared educational materials (the catechisms) to help Christian parents raise their children in the faith. They formulated worship orders and undertook efforts to educate pastors to carry on the proclamation of the gospel.

The wide vision of the church catholic that was maintained by Luther and his colleagues did not survive unscathed in succeeding generations. As Lutherans emigrated from their homelands to North America, some rebelled against the cold rationalism that dominated for a time European Lutheran state churches. Others misunderstood the "priesthood of all believers" and came to think that "church" was unnecessary. A private "God-and-me" piety flourished in places. It almost strangled any sense of Christians being knit together by God's Spirit into the whole body of Christ in the world, namely, the church.

The sixteenth-century affirmation of the catholic dimensions of the church was rooted not only in Scripture but also in the writings of the early centuries of the Christian era. The unity of the church was seen from the beginning as grounded in Christ.

An early church theologian named Tertullian in the third century expressed the broad unity of the church in this way: "We are a body knit together by the bond of piety, by unity of discipline, and by the contract of hope."[1] Later, in the early fifth century, Augustine elaborated on that concept, declaring that the catholicity of the church consists in its being the body of Christ in the world. This is reflected in its claim to teach the whole truth, and not selected fragments of it, and in its unbounded global scope and timeless dimensions.[2]

The rich heritage of understanding the wide implications of membership in the whole church and in this particular church that we call the ELCA sometimes has been clouded, however. Acknowledgment of the strategic importance of each community of faith—that is, each congregation—being gathered by Word and Sacrament does not preclude, and in fact even underscores, the urgency of affirming the churchliness of our common endeavors.

KEY PRINCIPLE OF UNITY

The primary principle of organization for the Evangelical Lutheran Church in America is unity: "The Evangelical Lutheran Church in America shall be *one* church [emphasis added]."[3] That crucial declaration is followed by confession of the source of this church's unity:

> This church recognizes that all power and authority in the Church belongs to the Lord Jesus Christ, its head. Therefore, all actions of this church by congregations, synods, and the churchwide organization shall be carried out under his rule and authority....[4]

Our church is committed to living and practicing the faith that we confess together. Therefore, we are dedicated to partnership and interdependence as a church. So we declare: "The congregations, synods, and churchwide organization shall act in accordance with the Confession of Faith set forth in chapter 2 of this constitution and with the Statement of Purpose set forth in chapter 4."[5]

The congregations, synods, and churchwide organization are each fully "church," as we noted earlier. Yet, we also noted that each is not, when separate from one another, the whole "church." These twin acknowledgments need to be held together by those who embrace the ecclesiology and polity of the Evangelical Lutheran Church in America.

That commitment to unity is underscored in the definition of membership in the Evangelical Lutheran Church in America. Indeed, who does belong to this church? "The members of this church shall be the baptized members of its congregations," the ELCA's churchwide constitutional provision on membership declares.[6] This means that the members of this church work together in their respective congregations, those 10,500 basic centers for mission through which members are nurtured in the Word of God as proclaimed and taught, washed and nourished through the sacraments, and sent into the journey of ministry in their daily lives. Those same members join hands with other members for the sake of the shared ministry that the people of this church undertake together through their respective synods and through the churchwide organization.

NATURE OF THIS CHURCH

Consider the way the basic "nature of the church" is defined in our church's governing documents:

> The Church exists both as an inclusive fellowship and as local congregations gathered for worship and Christian service.
> 1. Congregations find their fulfillment in the universal community of the Church, and the universal Church exists in and through congregations.
> 2. This church, therefore, derives its character and powers *both*
>   a. from the sanction and representation of its congregations and
>   b. from its inherent nature as an expression of the broader fellowship of the faithful.

3. In length, it acknowledges itself to be in the historic con-
    tinuity of the communion of saints; *[and]*
4. In breadth, it expresses the fellowship of believers and
    congregations in our day.[7]

Some individuals mistakenly have assumed that this 99-word
paragraph is the only statement of the ecclesiology of the Evangelical Lutheran Church in America, as contained in this church's
governing documents. It is not!

That provision itself, however, does have an interesting history. It was inserted as a new chapter in the ELCA constitution at
the final meeting of the Commission for a New Lutheran Church
(CNLC), held in Seattle June 23-25, 1986. The addition was made
in response to concerns expressed by synodical bishops of the
Lutheran Church in America (LCA) and by the LCA Executive
Council. They had worried publicly and officially about the "new
church" succumbing to "congregationalism." In the late spring
of 1986, LCA Bishop James R. Crumley Jr. wrote to LCA pastors,
arguing that "the solid embodiment in an ecclesiastical entity of
our self-understanding and self-identity as Lutherans" was crucial
for moving forward.[8]

The new chapter that was added at the Seattle CNLC meeting
was an exact quotation of Article IV, Section 2, in the constitution
of the Lutheran Church in America. Although a highly significant
addition, the text of the provision was inserted without debate and
with support of representatives of the two other merging bodies,
The American Lutheran Church (ALC) and the Association of
Evangelical Lutheran Churches (AELC).

SIGNIFICANT DEVELOPMENT

Although the provision on the Nature of the Church was copied
from the LCA constitution, its use in the ELCA constitution, when
coupled with the other constitutional definitions of the ELCA's
ecclesiology, represented a significant development. In both the governing documents and in practice, the Evangelical Lutheran Church
in America reflects a broader, deeper, and more historically and
confessionally grounded understanding of "church." Further, the
specific provision on the Nature of the Church acknowledges this
church's "inherent nature" as a reflection of the one, holy, catholic,

and apostolic church. Likewise, this church's "historic continuity" with the whole church universal, thereby, is underscored.

Further, this provision and related ones recognized that ecclesial (that is, churchly) reality does not reside exclusively in separate congregations, as necessary and strategic as each one is. After all, the whole ELCA is a church body, not merely a random association of self-contained, scattered communities of faith. Thus, the churchly reality abiding also in the expressions known as synods and the churchwide organization is embraced.

The crucial text of chapter 3 anchors the three primary expressions of this church—congregations, synods, and churchwide organization—within the context of the whole church of Jesus Christ.

If chapter 3 in the ELCA's churchwide constitution on the Nature of the Church (see text above) is viewed in isolation, it appears to present only a bipolar description of "church" as congregations and the whole church catholic. The ELCA's ecclesiology and polity, however, cannot be fully understood through exclusively focusing on that chapter. The chapter must be read in the context of ELCA constitution chapter 5 on organization,[9] chapter 6 on membership,[10] chapter 7 on ministry,[11] chapter 8 on relationships[12] (especially constitutional provision 8.11.), chapter 9 on congregations,[13] chapter 10 on synods,[14] chapter 11 on the churchwide organization,[15] and related provisions. Seen together, these sections offer a portrait of this church's ecclesiology and polity.

CONTINUITY WITH THE WHOLE CHURCH

In spite of the good foundation provided by chapter 3, perhaps the greatest danger in all the talk about a "new" church in the 1980s, in relation to the formation of the Evangelical Lutheran Church in America, was this—the creation of an impression of discontinuity, rather than continuity, with the whole church catholic and with the heritage of the predecessor church bodies. In relation to the wider context, an ELCA pastor and theologian named Carl E. Braaten warned, "No church can call itself Christian if it fails to preserve historical continuity with the apostolic origins of Christianity. . . . What we need is a concept of apostolicity which can freely acknowledge the historical difference between the apostolic period and our present situation without severing the vein of truth that connects the church of today with the apostolic mission."[16]

The conviction that the congregations, synods, and churchwide organization are each fully the church but, in themselves, not the whole church represents a gigantic step for some members and leaders throughout the Evangelical Lutheran Church in America.[17] The individualism reflected by certain immigrant strands of North American Lutheran history and the continuing individualistic spirit within U.S. society militate against a churchly awareness. Lutherans in America are not alone in facing this challenge, however. As the late Bishop Aulén wrote:

> The character of the church as "the mother who bears and fosters every Christian"[18] has often been obscured by the so-called individualistic movements. . . . [This] subjective reinterpretation of the idea of the church . . . places the individual Christian life as antecedent to the church and regards the church as an association of a greater or smaller number of individual Christians. . . . It has even been asserted that the essential meaning of the Reformation was that the emphasis was shifted from the church to the individual. That this is a gross misunderstanding is clear from the words already quoted from the Large Catechism concerning the church as mother. . . . If . . . individualistic Christianity is made to imply that the individual is independent of the church, that he [or she] is isolated from the fellowship with others, and that he [or she] is antecedent to the church, such an individualism is unrealistic and contrary to the condition under which faith lives. . . .

> [Nowhere] in the New Testament [do we] meet the idea that a person can qualify for membership in the church by any religious achievements. . . . Through the call of God the Christian is incorporated as a living member in the body of Christ . . . [and] is called to realize and actualize this membership. The relation between the gift of membership and the obligation it imposes meets us in the words of John 15:16: "You did not choose me, but I chose you and appointed you that you should go and bear fruit and that your fruit should abide. . . ."[19]

Luther envisioned the whole church as "a peculiar congregation" in the world. By means of this congregation, God brings people to Christ and teaches them the Word. Through the Word, God sustains the congregation in faith and brings forth the fruits of the Spirit in the world. Luther wrote:

> I believe that there is on earth a little holy flock or community of pure saints under one head, Christ. It is called together by the Holy Spirit in one faith, mind, and understanding. It possesses a variety of gifts, yet is united in love without sect or schism. Of this community I also am a part and member. . . . I was brought into it by the Holy Spirit and incorporated into it through the fact that I have heard and still hear God's Word. . . . Forgiveness is needed constantly, for although God's grace has been won by Christ, and holiness has been wrought by the Holy Spirit through God's Word in the unity of the Christian church, yet because we are encumbered with our flesh we are never without sin.

> Therefore everything in the Christian church is so ordered that we may daily obtain full forgiveness of sins through the Word and through signs [the sacraments] appointed to comfort and revive our consciences as long as we live.[20]

MORE THAN A SPIRITUAL CONCEPT

Conrad Bergendoff, one of the outstanding Lutheran theologians and church leaders of the twentieth century, observed: "For Luther the will of God is the preaching of the Word and this Word is living and active, producing faith and creating the people of God." The people of God are gathered by God's Spirit into the church, which is more than only a spiritual concept or an association of like-minded individuals. Dr. Bergendoff continued: "The element in which the church here [on earth] lives is a material and temporal one and no one can escape from it to a purer or timeless environment. Christ became incarnate not to save his people from the world but to save them in the world."[21]

Some have voiced the concern that this wider vision of the whole church may depreciate the importance of each congregation. The polity of this church, a few have suggested, looks at congregations as being of lesser value than that which was affirmed under some other Lutheran polities. That is not true. Such concerns reveal, however, a serious misunderstanding of the ecclesiology and polity reflected in the Evangelical Lutheran Church in America.

In reality, when one grasps a fuller sense of the whole church, the strategic importance of each congregation is underscored. Within each congregation is found fully the church; yet each congregation is fulfilled not in preoccupation only with its own "autonomous self," but rather in relationship to the whole body of Christ, the church.

We shall see the importance of this sense of unity and commitment to partnership in the life of your congregation and mine, and, indeed, throughout our whole church.

9

Not Alone

IN THE BEGINNING

Peter Stuyvesant was not happy. In fact, Stuyvesant, the Dutch colonial governor of what was called New Netherlands, was downright angry. How dare those Lutherans presume to bring a pastor into his territory! They even had the audacity to request formal permission for that pastor to lead worship in that Dutch colony.

Actually, the so-called Dutch Lutherans who had come to the area of what would become New York included more than folk from Holland. There also were German, Scandinavian, and Polish people. Some of them may have arrived as early as 1623 as part of the Dutch West India Company's commercial settlement. By 1649, many more had come and formed a congregation. When the first Lutheran pastor, Johannes Ernest Gutwasser, arrived in 1659, his presence caused such upheaval with the Dutch Reformed establishment that he was ordered deported by Governor Stuyvesant.

Just as was the case in the Netherlands at the time, the Reformed tradition was the state church in the New Netherlands colony. In the Netherlands, however, a degree of toleration had emerged. Such was not the case in settlements controlled by the Dutch West India Company. The practice of any other tradition was officially prohibited. When the English conquered the Dutch colony in 1664 and renamed it New York, Lutherans there gained religious liberty.

From those settlements along the Hudson River emerged what is now the oldest ELCA congregation, First Lutheran Church, established in 1649 at Albany, New York.

The Lutherans who settled in what became New York were not the first ones in North America. In 1619, King Christian IV of Denmark and Norway had sent two ships under the command of Jens Munk to what is now called Churchill on the Hudson Bay in Canada. A pastor, the Rev. Rasmus Jensen, was on that ill-fated expedition. Extreme cold, disease, and limited food took a severe toll. Pastor Jensen died in April 1620. Only Munk and two others survived; they returned to Denmark. No permanent Lutheran settlement emerged from that expedition.

Lutheranism was planted by the Danes, however, some years later in what then were called the Danish West Indies. From 1665 onward, a long line of Danish Lutheran clergy served on those islands that were purchased by the United States in 1917 and renamed the U.S. Virgin Islands. The second oldest ELCA congregation, Frederick Church, is located on St. Thomas.

Swedish immigrants came to the Delaware Valley in 1638 and established settlements in such places as Wilmington, Delaware, and Philadelphia, Pennsylvania. In 1639, the Rev. Reorus Torkillus came to serve among the Swedish immigrants. He became the first regular Lutheran pastor to serve in North America. Others followed him before those Swedish settlements went for several years without pastoral leadership. Further, a desire for English services emerged around the time of the Revolutionary War. Since English-speaking Lutheran pastors could not be found, some of those early Swedish Lutheran congregations called Anglican priests and became part of The Episcopal Church.

SUCCESSIVE WAVES OF IMMIGRATION

The Thirty Years' War in Europe (1618-1648) sparked extensive immigration to the New World. Thousands of people from especially southwestern Germany, an area hard-hit by the war, sought refuge in colonial America. They poured into Pennsylvania. Some of them turned southward and settled in Virginia or North Carolina. Still others entered Maryland, New York, and New Jersey. They came not only to escape the destruction of war; they also sought economic well-being, good land for farming, and better weather.

Successive waves of German Lutheran immigrants pressed farther westward in search of land. "Preaching stations" were established to serve those settlers. Already by the middle of the 1700s,

some 40,000 Lutherans were living in Pennsylvania. The need for
pastoral leadership was acute. Among the pioneer Lutheran pastors was the Rev. Daniel Falckner, who served in the community of
New Hanover from 1703 to 1708. (New Hanover Lutheran Church
is the third oldest ELCA congregation.) Another early pastor was
the Rev. Anthony Jacob Jenken, who also served in New Hanover
but, in addition, visited widely other German settlements as far
south as Virginia.

The Salzburger immigrants represented a special situation.
They were a persecuted Lutheran minority in their Roman Catholic homeland of Salzburg, a mountainous principality in what is
now Austria. In 1727, Archbishop Leopold Anthony von Firmian
declared, "I would rather have thorns and thistles on my fields
than Protestants in my land." He prohibited Lutheran worship,
arrested Lutheran leaders, and refused Lutherans the right to
baptism, marriage, and burial. On October 31, 1731, he ordered
all Protestants to leave Salzburg, unless they recanted and became
Roman Catholics.

About 30,000 refused to recant. They had to leave behind their
land, homes, and sometimes even family members. They jour-
neyed northward, singing in procession, "A Mighty Fortress Is Our
God." The Society for the Promotion of Christian Knowledge,
a benevolent organization in England, helped pay for the trans-
portation of the Salzburgers to a new colony being established in
Georgia by James Oglethorpe. The first contingent of Salzburgers
arrived in Charleston, South Carolina, in 1734. Two Lutheran pastors, John M. Boltzius and Israel C. Gronau, were in that group.
A settlement, called Ebenezer, was planted about 25 miles from
Savannah, Georgia. Eventually, the people of that settlement were
scattered to other German Lutheran communities in Georgia and
the Carolinas. Jerusalem Church remains today on the location of
the original Ebenezer settlement.

The rapid influx of Lutheran immigrants, especially in Pennsylvania and the surrounding states, presented a special challenge.
An extreme shortage of pastors prompted repeated requests to
Europe. As immigrants put down roots, they found themselves
facing a new situation. Lost in the transition were the structures
and systems of the European state-church pattern. New patterns
had to be found.

At the same time, a sense of freedom flourished. What had been seen as the oppressive spirit of their homeland—both political and religious—was gone. Now they found themselves free; for some, that even meant freedom *from* religion. A secular spirit flourished. Where interest in spiritual matters survived, a willingness to embrace a generic Protestantism emerged. From the beginning in a "new" land and at various points throughout succeeding decades and centuries, Lutheran identity was placed at risk or cast aside.

Further, the extreme shortage of pastors made communities vulnerable to imposters and opportunists—individuals who claimed to be pastors, yet were unable to teach the faith with integrity and unwilling to practice a piety appropriate for a spiritual leader. Some by their actions brought pain to communities and cynicism to those who had sought their spiritual guidance. So development of appropriate pastoral leadership was an immediate and ongoing concern for Lutherans in North America.

SEARCH FOR UNITY AND ORDER

In response to desperate pleas for pastors, the Rev. Henry Melchior Muhlenberg was sent in 1742 from Halle, Germany. His task was not only to serve the congregations in the Philadelphia area, to which he had been called. He also sought to bring unity and order to the scattered Lutheran congregations.

Out of his efforts and those of others, the first Lutheran "synod" was formed in 1748, generally known as the Ministerium of Pennsylvania and Adjacent States (see pages 38-40). That "synod" became one of the three dozen or so church organizations and church bodies that finally were united into the Evangelical Lutheran Church in America. Some of those early "synodical" organizations—in Ohio and Texas, for example—used the constitution of the Ministerium, changing only the name.

The establishment of that "synod" as the Ministerium of Pennsylvania proved extremely strategic for subsequent Lutheran identity in North America. The purpose of the synod was to provide for: (1) a regular, appropriately authorized, creditable ordination of properly prepared and approved candidates for pastoral ministry; (2) a common acceptance of the Lutheran Confessions as the basis for the beliefs, practices, and teachings of the Lutheran church; and (3) a common form of worship to reflect Lutheran unity. Determination of member congregations eventually rested within that synod too.

AS A CHURCH BODY

That first Lutheran church body in North America offered a foretaste of the future. Even as reflected then, likewise in current Lutheran experience, three central "powers" are crucial for the continuing unity of the Evangelical Lutheran Church in America as a church body within the whole body of Christ. Those three central "powers" or aspects of strategic authority are: the right to define what shall be this church's Confession of Faith; the right to define who shall serve as this church's ordained ministers; and the right to define the criteria for who shall be the congregations of this church.[1] The "authority" or "power" of this church for the exercise of these "rights" is essential for maintaining and expressing the unity of this church, as declared in its governing documents. We have seen how important these elements are in the criteria for recognition of ELCA congregations (see chapter 4).

From the early days of his work in colonial America, Pastor Muhlenberg also led in giving shape to congregational governance. He prepared constitutions for congregations. Lutheran congregational governance in North America, to a perhaps surprising degree, reflects even today the pattern that Pastor Muhlenberg carried with him from Lutheran congregations in Amsterdam and London on his way to America.

He also was instrumental in fostering a sense of Lutheran identity. This included conscientious efforts to educate pastors for succeeding generations. Originally, such candidates studied under a practicing pastor. Prior to ordination, they were examined publicly in a meeting of the "synod." The growing need both to provide an adequate supply of pastors and to maintain a healthy Lutheran witness in North America represented a gigantic challenge. Reliance on a European supply of clergy had been the initial practice. That proved neither a dependable nor sufficient source for pastors, given the rapidly expanding need. Hartwick Seminary in New York was opened in 1797, followed by the Lutheran Theological Seminary at Gettysburg, Pennsylvania, in 1826. Shortly thereafter, in 1830,

Lutheran Theological Southern Seminary in South Carolina began. Also in 1830, the Joint Synod of Ohio formed Lutheran Theological Seminary (now known as Trinity Lutheran Seminary in Columbus, Ohio). Other seminaries followed, often reflecting particular theological emphases, ethnic interests, regional focus, and even specific theological personalities.

IDENTITY SHAPED BY WORSHIP

Toward the end of Muhlenberg's life, he expressed the wish that "all Evangelical Lutheran Congregations in the North American States were united with one another, that all used the same order of service, the same hymn-book, and in good and evil days would show an active sympathy . . . with one another."[2] He understood the importance of worship and how worship shapes our identity as Lutherans, our sense of unity as a church, and our practice of faith in witness and service. Our public worship both reflects and nurtures our understanding of the faith and our identity as Lutherans. So decisions made about worship in a given congregation have long-term consequences, even for this whole church in generation after generation.

In our time, the crucial significance of worship for our church's life has been underscored for us in a major project of the Lutheran World Federation. That study was led by an ELCA pastor, the Rev. S. Anita Stauffer. As she explained, "For Christian worship there is no such thing as a *tabula rasa,* no blank slate. In matters of faith and liturgy we do not start from scratch. The starting point is already given in the death and resurrection of Christ, and in the Upper Room where the meaning of it all was made clear and the pattern of our own celebration of it was established."[3]

Dr. Stauffer also noted, "Worship needs not only to reflect the local [situation], but also the wider Christian community. . . . Christian worship . . . must be meaningful to those who worship in a given place. But at the same time, we must not lose Christ as the focus, or we will have cut off our roots and . . . [become] dead branches." After all, "everything human needs always to be critiqued by the light of the Gospel."[4]

When asked of their immediate concerns regarding the life of our church, members point often to what they see as core issues.

Between 1993 and 1995, for example, responses were invited from a broad sampling of ELCA pastors and members of congregations in a project that was known as the "Inquiry." What key concerns were expressed? Those interviewed spoke of the need to maintain a strong Lutheran identity, but at the same time to remain responsive to a changing society. They underscored the importance of mission, locally, domestically, and internationally. They pointed to the need for trusting relationships with leaders throughout this church. They emphasized the importance of leadership development and theological training.

The challenges that faced Pastor Muhlenberg and his colleagues remain with us even now, 250 years later.

CAME FROM SOMEPLACE

Except for the comparatively few members of the Evangelical Lutheran Church in America whose forebears were native to North America, all of the rest of us in the ELCA are descendants of immigrants, indentured servants, and slaves, or, in some cases, are first-generation immigrants.

Two chief periods of heavy immigration shaped Lutheran church life in North America. The first occurred in the mid-1700s and brought many Germans and some others into the colonies or, later, initial states in the new nation. The newer immigrants moved westward in search of land into Ohio and beyond.

The second era of substantial immigration began in the late 1830s and extended throughout much of the nineteenth century. That era, too, was characterized by substantial German immigration but also by heavy Scandinavian immigration, especially to parts of the Upper Midwest (Illinois, Wisconsin, Iowa, Minnesota, and the Dakotas).

The second wave of immigration brought some 1.75 million Scandinavian people. Half of them came from Sweden and about a third from Norway. Historians report, however, that most left their church membership behind. The Norwegian branches of U.S. Lutheranism succeeded to a greater degree than the other ethnic groups in gathering immigrants. About 30 percent of the Norwegian immigrants became part of the Lutheran church; for Swedish immigrants, the number amounted to 20 percent, and for Danes, only seven percent, in spite of the diligent formation of Danish "folk schools," short-term institutions with a strong cultural emphasis.[5] The need for outreach has been a concern since the earliest days for Lutherans in North America.

The type of people who emigrated had an impact on both Lutheran church life and U.S. social development. For example, Norwegian immigrants to the Upper Midwest were chiefly farmers, fisherfolk, and laborers. Wealthy people rarely emigrated. Those who came generally represented the poor working class in Norway. They sought in America economic well-being and freedom. Many of them had been influenced by the religious "populism" of the reform movement led by Hans Nilson Hauge (1771-1824) in Norway. They and their descendants—as well as other Scandinavian and German immigrants—found a comfortable companion to religious populism in the political Populist Movement that flourished, especially in Wisconsin, Minnesota, and North Dakota, in the late 1800s and early 1900s.

Many Finnish immigrants became involved in iron-ore mining and shipping on the Great Lakes to the eastern steel plants. Others found work in forestry. They settled in the Upper Peninsula of Michigan as well as parts of Ohio, Minnesota, and elsewhere. Strong ethnic ties have been maintained by many Finnish descendants. Similar observations could be made of other immigrant groups.

The one non-geographic synod in the ELCA is the Slovak Zion Synod. That synod has emphasized the ethnic heritage of its members and fostered strong family and cultural ties with Slovakia in eastern Europe.

People of African American heritage have been a part of Lutheran church life in North America since colonial days and now number some 51,000 in ELCA congregations.

In recent years, there has been significant growth in the Hispanic or Latino population in the United States. Substantial immigration also has occurred from Asian countries or Pacific Islands. Congregations of the ELCA list about 28,000 Hispanic or Latino members, 22,500 Asian American members, and 7,000 American Indian and Alaskan Native members. To some degree, these population shifts have shown themselves within the membership of

ELCA congregations. The immigration of more recent years, in a way, continues the pattern of previous eras.

SHIFTS TO ENGLISH

In spite of shifts to English by some congregations from the early days of Lutherans in North America, the mix of many languages for Lutherans persisted. Many immigrant groups maintained worship in their native languages into the early twentieth century. Eventually, language transition ceased to be an option. Younger members wanted English. Further, during World War I, the change was immediate for most congregations that had been using German. The shift to English for many other congregations occurred in the 1920s. Yet much variety can still be found on Sunday mornings in ELCA congregations.

In the mid-1990s, 520 congregations reported using, at least occasionally, languages other than English. Among the languages used were: Spanish in 185 congregations; Korean in 16; Mandarin, 14; Latvian, 12; Cantonese, 10; Hmong, 7; Amharic, 6; Lao, 6; Taiwanese, 5; Inupiat, 5; Estonian, 5; Vietnamese, 5; Wendish, 2; Tai, 2; Navajo, 2; Japanese, 2; Cambodian, 2; Arabic and Yoruba, 1. Fifty-four congregations said German was used, at least occasionally. Other languages included Finnish, 26; Slovak, 16; Norwegian, 7; Swedish, 7; Danish, 5; and Hungarian, 1. Signing was done in 111 congregations.

The Evangelical Lutheran Church in America, both in the governing documents and in practice, reflects an understanding of the catholic nature of the church, meaning the church is universal and spans all space and time. Furthermore, the conviction that the gospel is for all people is demonstrated in the ministries of ELCA congregations, synods, and churchwide programs. The fact that Lutherans largely represent an immigrant church provides an apt reminder of the need for continuing outreach, particularly in the midst of the growing diversity of U.S. society.

From the beginning, a commitment was made in the ELCA to a broad scope of ministry, reflecting the Great Commission of our Lord. As part of that commitment, at least one-fifth of new congregations have been planted in ethnic communities.

Acknowledging the variety of people who have been a part of the Lutheran movement in North America and demonstrating an awareness of the growing diversity within U.S. society, a commitment was made in the ELCA, at its formation, to being inclusive. This included specific representational goals for synodical and churchwide assemblies, councils, boards, and committees. For representation, at least 60 percent of the voting members are to be laypersons, half of them women and half of them men. At least ten percent of the voting members are to be persons of color or persons whose primary language is other than English.

Such a commitment to being inclusive was undertaken in response to the gospel. Confessing that the gospel is for all people, the ELCA seeks to be an inclusive church even in the midst of divisions in society. If viewed in isolation, the representational principles might appear to be only a sociological gimmick. Instead, even the principles themselves are grounded in the conviction that we are called to heal divisions and proclaim reconciliation for all. The representational principles themselves may be a way through which God's Spirit may work to lift up new leadership and to yield wholesome results in the life of all expressions of this church.

All leaders in the life of this church are summoned to be servants not only in their words but also in their patterns of life and manners of leadership. They are called in our governing documents as a church to understand that "their accountability [is] to the Triune God, to the whole church, to each other, and to the organization of this church in which they have been asked to serve."[6] Further, they are to be good stewards of the work and resources entrusted to them for the ministry of this whole church.[7]

Together with a vast array of others from many lands and ethnic heritages, then, we are summoned to be one church in mission—the mission that God has given us in our time.

10

All One Body

MARCHING WITH THE CROSS

In the congregation of my childhood, the hymn of Sabine Baring-Gould occasionally would be sung in worship. The images of World War II battles, the struggles of the Korean conflict in the early 1950s, and the year-after-year tensions of the Cold War provided the context in my early years. The hymn put the concerns of Christian witness and service in terms of battle.

> *Onward, Christian soldiers,*
>   *Marching as to war,*
> *With the cross of Jesus*
>   *Going on before:*
> *Christ, the Royal Master,*
>   *Leads against the foe;*
> *Forward into battle,*
>   *See, his banners go.[1]*

The hymn was written in 1864 for a Sunday school procession with cross and banners in Yorkshire, England. The hymn reflected vivid awareness of the high cost of being disciples. It was written within a significant context for the whole church. An understanding of the importance of Christian mission on a global scale was growing rapidly in the 1800s and early 1900s. So, people sang:

> *Like a mighty army*
>   *Moves the Church of God. . . .*

and

> *Crowns and thrones may perish,*
> *Kingdoms rise and wane,*
> *But the Church of Jesus*
> *Constant will remain. . . .*

We do not sing that hymn very much anymore. Although the hymn was in *Lutheran Book of Worship*, it disappeared from many other hymnbooks published in the past quarter century. It was judged too militaristic. The text is seen by some as not reflecting appropriately the Prince of Peace. Its words often are viewed as not offering wholesome witness by followers of the one who came "not to be served but to serve, and to give his life a ransom for many" (Mark 10:45).

In the second stanza of that hymn, we may recall an apt description of our life together in the Evangelical Lutheran Church in America. Given our unity as part of the Lutheran communion of churches and our commitment to partnership in the mission God has set before us as members of the ELCA, we can say:

> *We are not divided,*
> *All one body we,*
> *One in hope and doctrine,*
> *One in charity.*

The three primary "expressions" of this church—congregations, synods, and churchwide organization—practice what Martin Luther identified as marks of the whole church. Luther described these marks as the Word, Baptism, the Lord's Supper, the keys (confession and absolution), the ministry, prayer, and suffering.[2] Indeed, as the late Herman A. Preus, for many years a theological professor at Luther Seminary in St. Paul, Minnesota, wrote, "Suffering and cross-bearing are . . . recognized as the normal way of the Christian life and the necessary means of purging out self-dependence and of driving one to Christ, who suffered before us and for us."[3]

CHURCH INCARNATE IN ORGANIZATION

The church in history always will have an organizational pattern. Even so, however, as we saw in chapter 7, Lutherans historically have never considered a specific church order necessary. We Lutherans have placed primary emphasis not on structures, but rather on faithfulness in apostolic witness and commitment to God's mission in the world. We "have defined the essence of Christianity in terms of proper understanding of the Gospel of grace, rather than in terms of community structures," Dr. Philip Hefner of the Lutheran School of Theology at Chicago has noted.[4] Affirmation in the creeds of the apostolic nature of the church represents "the church's acknowledgment that it lives by what it has received and it is accountable to what it has received."[5]

Human order and organization in the common life of the church on earth are essential, not for their own sake but for the sake of the gospel. As Eric W. Gritsch and Robert W. Jenson, two widely regarded Lutheran theologians and professors, observed:

> Luther's keen sense of Christian realism permeated not only confessional arguments concerning the unity of the church, but also its reality. The church, like the individual Christian, is "simultaneously righteous and sinful" (*simul iustus et peccator*). Ecclesiastical purity is not a moral but a functional phenomenon: as long as the church is guided by the Holy Spirit, mediated by Word and Sacrament, it will remain pure in its earthly purpose to be the instrument of God's promise of salvation without the merit of good works.[6]

> As a community extended through time, the church will be organized, whether it wants to be or not. . . . God gathers people and . . . this gathering, the church, creates an organization in order to carry out its mission.[7]

"Organization is necessary if an association wants to be capable of action toward the inside and toward the outside . . . ," Lutheran theologian Werner Elert wrote, in commenting on the essential development of church structure.[8] Further, he observed that, as early as 1523, "Luther does not speak of the local congregation as being . . . self-sufficient. The practical expression of his conviction is seen in the fact that visitations were carried out. In particular, the observance of the 'evangelical doctrine' (*doctrina evangelica*) is not the concern of the individual congregation [alone]; it is the concern of all those who profess this doctrine."[9]

We see, then, that organizational structure is not viewed as a matter of indifference. Part of the reason for this is a Lutheran recognition of human nature; another part emerges from a Lutheran acknowledgment of the "two realms" of God's activity in the world. Luther understood that God works both through human order or law, on the one hand, and through the gospel, on the other. He acknowledged the need for both secular authority, exercised in the state for public peace, security, and justice, and the confession of faith, nurtured through the church. The function of government and human order is to punish evildoers and protect the people and families in peace, he taught. While the state seeks to maintain human concord and well-being, the task of spiritual authority is to foster faith in the preaching of the gospel. Through the gospel, God establishes dominion in human hearts.

NOT A HEAVENLY VESTIBULE

Lutherans and others sometimes forget that the church as a human community or institution exists under both "realms." Yet, as Dr. Gerhard Forde of Luther Seminary in St. Paul, Minnesota, succinctly observed, "The church as a sociological organization is not an eschatological [or heavenly] vestibule into which one can prematurely escape from politics," that is, the processes of human order.[10] Within the human community of the church, however, Jesus exercises his rule of grace through the church's ongoing witness. The living Christ does not create faith by a direct revelation to an individual or some mystical relationship apart from the preaching of the Word and the action of the sacraments.

Dr. Gritsch emphasized the "both-and" dimensions of our life as part of the church. He wrote, "The church . . . is the community that lives in both realms—that of the Law with its call for order and that of the Gospel with its promise of a new creation. Lutherans know how difficult it is to live in both realms. They, like other Christians, have been tempted to focus solely on law and order, and at other times to idealize life lived in the Gospel."[11]

Further, Dr. Gritsch recalls that "Christian tradition likes to compare the church to a ship tossed about in the rough seas of the world." With that image in mind, we need to remember, however, that:

Members of the church are not on a pleasure cruise, they are
the crew, and are obligated to do everything in their power to
keep the ship afloat. The ship is in constant touch with its real
captain, Christ. Gathering every seventh day for the past two mil-
lennia, Christians have been strengthened in their discipleship
by Christ's presence in Word and Sacrament, liturgy and prayer,
and meditation and celebration. But there is always Monday with
its struggles between Law and Gospel. Using another image, the
church is a halfway house between the two realms. "Now we are
only halfway pure and holy," Luther told his congregation. "The
Holy Spirit must continue to work in us through the Word, daily
granting forgiveness until we attain to that life where there will
be no more [need for] forgiveness," [wrote Luther in the Large
Catechism].[12] One must, therefore, remain vigilant and be able to
distinguish properly between sin and grace, Law and Gospel, and
church and world.[13]

SOME ANSWERS

We now have some answers to our original question, "What is
happening in the Evangelical Lutheran Church in America?" Obviously a great deal, for as members of the ELCA, we walk together
in witness and service.

In our journey, we approach the table of our Lord. We kneel
and the pastor gives us the bread of Holy Communion. We
respond, "Amen." With that "Amen," we acknowledge that our
sacramental eating is much more than a private experience of
personal piety. We are declaring that we are receiving the gift of
Christ's presence. We also recognize those around us as part of the
body of Christ. We are confessing that we will go from that table
as the body of Christ in the world. And we are embracing the body
of Christ, the church, that surrounds and upholds us in the faith.

The unity of the whole church and of the Evangelical Lutheran
Church in America is given by the Holy Spirit. We are called in our
time to give that unity form and expression. We do so in the ways
we work together for the sake of the gospel. Indeed, we can say:

> *We are not divided,*
>   *All one body we,*
> *One in hope and doctrine,*
>   *One in charity.*

This claim must not be an idle one. Too much is at stake. God summons us together to march across the threshold of a new century as a living, breathing, and working body—a precious part of the church, which is the body of Christ in the world.

We are called, under the cross, to march as one great cloud of witnesses. You and the members of your congregation journey as pilgrims within the church of Christ. You are a strategic member of the part of the church that we know as the Evangelical Lutheran Church in America. With believers throughout the whole world, you live in faith, witnessing and serving in Christ's name. Indeed,

All one body we. . . .

Notes

CHAPTER 1

1. This listing is based on the roster of congregations of the Evangelical Lutheran Church in America as maintained by the Office of the Secretary of the ELCA in Chicago.
2. The most complete history to date of the formation of the Evangelical Lutheran Church in America is *Anatomy of a Merger* by Edgar R. Trexler (Minneapolis: Augsburg, 1991). A brief and readable summary of the history of the three uniting churches is *All These Lutherans* by Todd W. Nichol (Minneapolis: Augsburg, 1986). An account of the background of The American Lutheran Church is *Church Roots: Stories of Nine Immigrant Groups That Became The American Lutheran Church*, edited by Charles P. Lutz (Minneapolis: Augsburg, 1985). *Commitment to Unity* by W. Kent Gilbert (Philadelphia: Fortress, 1988) provides a comprehensive history of the Lutheran Church in America. Insights into the events surrounding the formation of the Association of Evangelical Lutheran Churches are found in *Memoirs in Exile: Confessional Hope and Institutional Conflict* by John H. Tietjen (Minneapolis: Fortress, 1990).

CHAPTER 2

1. The plan for such a commission was put together by what was known from 1978 as the Committee on Lutheran Unity. (An earlier committee had done preliminary work on the possibilities for church union.) After much debate, the Committee on Lutheran Unity proposed a 70-member commission. Some committee members had favored a smaller group to save money and achieve greater efficiency in decision-making. Within the commission, 31 were to be elected by the biennial convention of the Lutheran Church in America (LCA), 31 by the general convention of The American Lutheran Church (ALC), and eight by the convention of the Association of Evangelical Lutheran Churches (AELC).

A pattern of representation proportionate to the relative size of the uniting churches was not followed. Part of the reason for that arose from the anxiety of some in the ALC (with 2.25 million members) that the LCA (with 2.85 million members) could dominate the negotiations and control the outcome. By allocating disproportionately large representation to the AELC (with 100,000 members) and by agreeing to equal representation for both the LCA and ALC, it was assumed that voting along the lines of predecessor church bodies would be avoided. To a large degree, that proved to be true throughout the four years in which Commission for a New Lutheran Church (CNLC) members did their work. That may have been less the result of the allocated representation and more a matter of individual convictions.

2. The same resolution was adopted by the three conventions of the uniting churches in 1982 by an overwhelming vote: ALC–897 yes, 87 no; LCA–611 yes, 11 no; and AELC–136 yes, 0 no. The people in all three conventions (ALC in San Diego, California; LCA in Louisville, Kentucky; and AELC in Cleveland, Ohio) sang, following the announcement of the vote, "The Church's One Foundation."

3. As a member of the committee appointed to propose possible names for the "new" Lutheran church, I wrote the rationale for using the name *Evangelical Lutheran Church* and including identification of this church's primary territory within the name, just as is the case for the Evangelical Lutheran Church in Canada and other Lutheran churches throughout the world. Quotations in this section are from the "Report of the Ad Hoc Committee on [the] Name for the New Lutheran Church." The five-member committee presented the report to the September 23-27, 1985, meeting of the Commission for a New Lutheran Church.

CHAPTER 3

1. See chapter 2, "Confession of Faith," in *Constitution, Bylaws, and Continuing Resolutions of the Evangelical Lutheran Church in America*, 2005 edition, page 19. The bold face introductions to each section have been inserted into the text to provide an outline of the basic point of each paragraph.

2. Explanation to the First Article of the Apostles' Creed, *A Contemporary Translation of Luther's Small Catechism*, introduction and translation by Timothy J. Wengert (Minneapolis: Augsburg Fortress, 1994), page 25.

3. Explanation to the Second Article of the Apostles' Creed, *Luther's Small Catechism*, page 27.

4. Explanation to the Third Article of the Apostles' Creed, *Luther's Small Catechism*, page 29.
5. *Lutheran Book of Worship*, pages 54-55.
6. Article VII, "The Church," Augsburg Confession, *The Book of Concord*, translated and edited by Theodore G. Tappert (Philadelphia: Fortress, 1959), page 32.
7. Article IV, "Justification," Augsburg Confession, *Book of Concord*, page 30.
8. Article V, "The Office of the Ministry," Augsburg Confession, *Book of Concord*, page 31.

CHAPTER 4

1. "O Day Full of Grace," stanza five, hymn 161, *Lutheran Book of Worship*, text copyright 1978.
2. Article VII, "The Church," Augsburg Confession, *Book of Concord*, page 32.
3. Provision 9.11. in the ELCA churchwide constitution (2005 edition), page 60.
4. "Toward a Lutheran Understanding of Communion," a document of the Department for Theology and Studies of the Lutheran World Federation (Geneva: Lutheran World Federation, 1996), page 7.
5. See provision 9.21., ELCA churchwide constitution (2005 edition), page 60.
6. Provision 9.41., ELCA churchwide constitution (2005 edition), page 62. The same text is found in required provision *C4.03. in the Model Constitution for Congregations as contained in the ELCA churchwide constitution, pages 219-220.
7. Required provision *C8.02. in the Model Constitution for Congregations, contained in the ELCA churchwide constitution (2005 edition), page 224.
8. Required provision *C8.04. in the Model Constitution for Congregations, contained in the ELCA churchwide constitution (2005 edition), page 225.
9. The statistics and other data about ELCA congregations and members cited in this chapter are based on information compiled by the Office of the Secretary and the Research and Evaluation section in the ELCA churchwide organization.
10. Provision 7.21., ELCA churchwide constitution (2005 edition), page 27.
11. Provision 7.22., ELCA churchwide constitution (2005 edition), page 27.

12. Article XIV, "Order in the Church," Augsburg Confession, *Book of Concord*, page 36.
13. Philip Hefner, "Basic Elements of the Church's Life," *Christian Dogmatics*, Volume 2, edited by Carl E. Braaten and Robert W. Jenson (Philadelphia: Fortress, 1984), pages 224-225.
14. Herbert F. Brokering, *"I" Opener: Eighty Parables* (St. Louis: Concordia, 1974), page 31.
15. *Lutheran Book of Worship*, page 68.

CHAPTER 5

1. Provision 10.21., ELCA churchwide constitution (2005 edition), page 77.
2. Provision 3.02., ELCA churchwide constitution (2005 edition), page 20.
3. *The Journals of Henry Melchior Muhlenberg*, Volume 1, translated by Theodore G. Tappert and John W. Doberstein (Philadelphia: Muhlenberg Press and the Evangelical Lutheran Ministerium of Pennsylvania and Adjacent States, 1942), page 445.
4. According to provision †S6.03. in the Constitution for Synods, each synod, in partnership with the churchwide organization, is to bear primary responsibility for the oversight of the life and mission of this church in the territory of the synod. In fulfillment of that role, the synod is to:
   a. Provide for the pastoral care of congregations, ordained ministers, associates in ministry, deaconesses, and diaconal ministers of this church in this synod, including:
      (1) approving candidates for the ordained ministry . . . ;
      (2) authorizing ordinations and ordaining on behalf of this church;
      (3) approving associates in ministry, deaconesses, and diaconal ministers of this church . . . ;
      (4) authorizing the commissioning of associates in ministry, the consecration of deaconesses, and the consecration of diaconal ministers of this church; and
      (5) consulting in the calling process for ordained ministers, associates in ministry, deaconesses, and diaconal ministers.
   b. Provide for leadership recruitment, preparation, and support in accordance with churchwide standards and policies, including:
      (1) nurturing and supporting congregations and lay leaders;
      (2) seeking and recruiting qualified candidates for the rostered ministries of this church;

(3) making provision for pastoral care, call or appointment review, and guidance;

(4) encouraging and supporting persons on the rosters of this church in stewardship of their abilities, care of self, and pursuit of continuing education to undergird their effectiveness of service; and

(5) supporting recruitment of leaders for this church's colleges, universities, seminaries, and social ministry organizations.

c. Plan for the mission of this church in this synod, initiating and developing policy and implementing programs, consistent with churchwide policy, including . . . :

(1) development of new ministries, redevelopment of existing ministries, and support and assistance in the conclusion, if necessary, of a particular ministry;

(2) leadership and encouragement of congregations in their evangelism efforts;

(3) development of relationships to and participation in planning for the mission of social ministry organizations and ministries; [and]

(4) encouragement of financial support for the work of this church by individuals and congregations. . . .

d. Promote interdependent relationships among congregations, synods, and the churchwide organization, and enter into partnership with other synods in the region.

e. Participate in churchwide programs and develop support for the ministry of the churchwide organization.

f. Support relationships with and provide partnership funding on behalf of colleges, universities, and campus ministries.

g. Foster relationships with and provide partnership funding on behalf of social ministry organizations.

h. Maintain relationships with and provide partnership funding on behalf of seminaries and continuing education centers.

i. Foster supporting relationships with camps and other outdoor ministries.

j. Foster organizations for youth, women, and men, and organizations for language or ethnic communities.

k. Provide for discipline of congregations, ordained ministers, and persons on the official lay rosters; as well as for termination of call, appointment, adjudication, and appeals. . . .

l. Elect [voting] members of the Churchwide Assembly. . . .

5. Provision †S8.12. in the Constitution for Synods outlines the

responsibilities of each synodical bishop:

As this synod's pastor, the bishop shall be an ordained minister of Word and Sacrament who shall:

a. Preach, teach, and administer the sacraments in accord with the Confession of Faith of this church.

b. Have primary responsibility for the ministry of Word and Sacrament in this synod and its congregations, providing pastoral care and leadership for this synod, its congregations, its ordained ministers, and its other rostered leaders.

c. Exercise solely this church's power to ordain (or provide for the ordination by another synodical bishop of) approved candidates who have received and accepted a properly issued, duly attested letter of call for the office of ordained ministry.

d. Commission (or provide for the commissioning of) approved candidates who have received and accepted a properly issued, duly attested letter of call for service as associates in ministry; consecrate (or provide for the consecration of) approved candidates who have received and accepted a properly issued, duly attested letter of call for service as deaconesses of the ELCA; and consecrate (or provide for the consecration of) approved candidates who have received and accepted a properly issued, duly attested letter of call for service as diaconal ministers of this church.

e. Attest letters of call for persons called to serve congregations in the synod, letters of call for persons called by the Synod Council, and letters of call for persons called by the Church Council on the roster of this synod.

f. Install (or provide for the installation of): (1) the pastors of all congregations of this synod; (2) ordained ministers called to extraparish service within this church; and (3) persons serving in the other rostered ministries within this synod.

g. Exercise leadership in the mission of this church and in so doing: (1) interpret and advocate the mission and theology of the whole church; (2) lead in fostering support for and commitment to the mission of this church within this synod; [and] (3) coordinate the use of the resources available to this synod as it seeks to promote the health of this church's life and witness in the areas served by this synod. . . .

h. Practice leadership in strengthening the unity of the church. . . .

i. Oversee and administer the work of this synod and in so doing . . . , serve as the president of the synod corporation, and be the chief executive and administrative officer of this synod. . . .

j. Ensure that the constitution and bylaws of the synod and of
the churchwide organization are duly observed within this
synod, and that the actions of the synod in conformity there-
with are carried into effect. . . .

k. Provide for preparation and maintenance of synodical rosters
containing: (1) the names and addresses of all ordained ministers of this synod and a record of the calls under which they are
serving or the date on which they become retired or disabled;
and (2) the names and addresses of all other rostered persons
of this synod and a record of the positions to which they have
been called or the date on which they become retired or disabled. . . .

l. Provide for preparation and maintenance of a register of the
congregations of this synod and the names of the laypersons
who have been elected to represent them. . . .

6. Article XXVIII, Apology to the Augsburg Confession, *Book of
Concord*, page 283.

7. Article XXVIII, "Power of Bishops," Augsburg Confession, *Book of
Concord*, page 90.

CHAPTER 6

1. Provision 8.11., ELCA churchwide constitution (2005 edition), page
52.

2. Provision 11.11., ELCA churchwide constitution (2005 edition),
page 85.

3. Churchwide constitution provision 4.02. expresses the Statement of
Purpose for the congregations, synods, and churchwide organiza-
tion of the Evangelical Lutheran Church in America:
To participate in God's mission, this church shall:

a. Proclaim God's saving Gospel of justification by grace for
Christ's sake through faith alone, according to the apostolic
witness in the Holy Scripture, preserving and transmitting the
Gospel faithfully to future generations.

b. Carry out Christ's Great Commission by reaching out to all
people to bring them to faith in Christ and by doing all ministry with a global awareness consistent with the understanding
of God as Creator, Redeemer, and Sanctifier of all.

c. Serve in response to God's love to meet human needs, caring
for the sick and the aged, advocating dignity and justice for
all people, working for peace and reconciliation among the

nations, and standing with the poor and powerless and committing itself to their needs.

d. Worship God in proclamation of the Word and administration of the sacraments and through lives of prayer, praise, thanksgiving, witness, and service.

e. Nurture its members in the Word of God so as to grow in faith and hope and love, to see daily life as the primary setting for the exercise of their Christian calling, and to use the gifts of the Spirit for their life together and for their calling in the world.

f. Manifest the unity given to the people of God by living together in the love of Christ and by joining with other Christians in prayer and action to express and preserve the unity which the Spirit gives.

4. Provision 11.12., ELCA churchwide constitution (2005 edition), page 85.

5. As expressed in churchwide constitutional provision 4.03., the general purposes of the Evangelical Lutheran Church in America are to:

a. Receive, establish, and support those congregations, ministries, organizations, institutions, and agencies necessary to carry out God's mission through this church.

b. Encourage and equip all members to worship, learn, serve, and witness; to fulfill their calling to serve God in the world; and to be stewards of the earth, their lives, and the Gospel.

c. Call forth, equip, certify, set apart, supervise, and support an ordained ministry of Word and sacrament and such other forms of ministry that will enable this church to fulfill its mission.

d. Seek unity in faith and life with all Lutherans within its boundaries and be ready to enter union negotiations whenever such unity is manifest.

e. Foster Christian unity by participating in ecumenical activities, contributing its witness and work and cooperating with other churches which confess God the Father, Son, and Holy Spirit.

f. Develop relationships with communities of other faiths for dialogue and common action.

g. Lift its voice in concord and work in concert with forces for good, to serve humanity, cooperating with church and other groups participating in activities that promote justice, relieve misery, and reconcile the estranged.

h. Produce and publish worship materials for corporate, family, and personal use and resources for education, witness, service, and stewardship.

i.   Establish and maintain theological seminaries, schools, colleges, universities, and other educational institutions to equip people for leadership and service in church and society.

j.   Assure faithfulness to this church's confessional position and purpose and provide for resolution of disputes.

k.   Publish a periodical and make use of the arts and public communication media to proclaim the Gospel and to inform, interpret, and edify.

l.   Study social issues and trends, work to discover the causes of oppression and injustice, and develop programs of ministry and advocacy to further human dignity, freedom, justice, and peace in the world.

m.   Establish, support, and recognize institutions and agencies that minister to people in spiritual and temporal needs.

n.   Work with civil authorities in areas of mutual endeavor, maintaining institutional separation of church and state in a relation of functional interaction.

o.   Provide structures and decision-making processes for this church that foster mutuality and interdependence and that involve people in making decisions that affect them.

p.   Support the mission of this church by arranging for and encouraging financial contributions for its work, management of its resources, and processes of planning and evaluation. . . .

6.   The specific functions of the churchwide organization are defined in this way in churchwide constitutional provision 11.21. The churchwide organization is to:

a.   Undergird the worship life of this church as the Word of God is preached and the sacraments are administered.

b.   Provide resources to equip members to worship, learn, serve, and witness in their ministry in daily life.

c.   Support and establish policy for this church's mission and coordinate planning and evaluation for that mission throughout the world, including participation with other churches.

d.   Witness to the Word of God in Christ by united efforts in proclaiming the Gospel, responding to human need, caring for the sick and suffering, working for justice and peace, and providing guidance to members on social matters.

e.   Foster interdependent relationships among congregations, synods, and the churchwide organization to implement the mission of this whole church.

f.   Provide for the ordained ministry and other rostered ministries of this church.

g. Oversee and establish policy for this church's relationship to seminaries, colleges, universities, schools, and other education endeavors, and provide support as appropriate.

h. Establish and reflect this church's ecumenical stance and its relationship to other churches, and direct this church's policy for relationship with persons of other faiths.

i. Develop and administer policies for this church's relationship to social ministry organizations and cooperate with public and private agencies that enhance human dignity and justice.

j. Determine and implement policy for this church's relationship to governments.

k. Provide for a comprehensive financial support system for this church's mission and for the administration of financial resources necessary for fulfillment of the particular responsibilities of the churchwide organization.

l. Provide planned giving opportunities for the financial support of this church, its congregations, synods, agencies, and institutions through the establishment of a foundation.

m. Provide pension and other benefits plans for this church.

n. Provide a church publishing house.

o. Provide archives for the retention of its valuable records, and coordinate archival activity in the synods, regions, institutions, and agencies of this church.

p. Provide and monitor a system of discipline, appeals, and adjudication.

q. Establish and operate other programs and activities, as determined by this church, on behalf of and in support of the congregations and synods of this church.

7. See provision 5.01.f., ELCA churchwide constitution (2005 edition), pages 23-24.

8. Provision 11.32., ELCA churchwide constitution (2005 edition), page 86.

9. Provision 11.33., ELCA churchwide constitution (2005 edition), page 86.

10. Provision 11.34., ELCA churchwide constitution (2005 edition), page 86.

11. Bylaw 15.11.02., ELCA churchwide constitution (2005 edition), page 106.

12. Continuing resolution 16.12.A05., ELCA churchwide constitution (2005 edition), page 115.

13. Continuing resolution 16.12.B05., ELCA churchwide constitution (2005 edition), pages 116-117.

14. Continuing resolution 16.12.C05., ELCA churchwide constitution (2005 edition), pages 117-120.
15. Continuing resolution 16.12.C05., ELCA churchwide constitution (2005 edition), page 119.
16. Continuing resolution 16.12.D05., ELCA churchwide constitution (2005 edition), pages 121-123.
17. Continuing resolution 16.12.E05., ELCA churchwide constitution (2005 edition), pages 123-124.
18. Provision 16.31., ELCA churchwide constitution (2005 edition), page 124.
19. Provision 16.41., ELCA churchwide constitution (2005 edition), page 126.
20. Continuing resolution 17.21.A05., ELCA churchwide constitution (2005 edition), pages 129-130.
21. Provision 17.31., ELCA churchwide constitution (2005 edition), page 130.
22. Provision 17.41., ELCA churchwide constitution (2005), pages 131-132.
23. Continuing resolution 17.41.B05., ELCA churchwide constitution (2005 edition), pages 133-134.
24. Provision 17.51., ELCA churchwide constitution (2005), page 134.
25. Provision 17.61., ELCA churchwide constitution (2005), page 135.
26. Provision 8.31., ELCA churchwide constitution (2005), page 53.
27. Provision 8.31.01., ELCA churchwide constitution (2005), page 53.
28. Provision 8.31.03., ELCA churchwide constitution (2005), page 53.
29. Provision 8.31.04., ELCA churchwide constitution (2005), page 53.
30. Provision 8.31.06., ELCA churchwide constitution (2005), page 54.
31. These quotations are based on notes of an interview with the Rev. Phyllis B. Anderson, at that time director for theological education in the ELCA Division for Ministry (February 17, 1997).
32. Provision 8.32., ELCA churchwide constitution (2005), page 54.
33. Bylaw 8.32.01., ELCA churchwide constitution (2005), page 54.
34. Bylaw 8.32.02., ELCA churchwide constitution (2005 edition), page 54.
35. Bylaw 8.32.05., ELCA churchwide constitution (2005 edition), page 55.
36. Provision 8.33., ELCA churchwide constitution (2005 edition), page 55.

CHAPTER 7

1. Article VII, "The Church," Augsburg Confession, *Book of Concord*, page 32.
2. Richard P. McBrien, "Church," *The Westminster Dictionary of Christian Theology*, edited by Alan Richardson and John Bowden (Philadelphia: The Westminster Press, 1983), page 108.
3. Apology to the Augsburg Confession, *Book of Concord*, page 170.
4. Apology to the Augsburg Confession, *Book of Concord*, page 171 and 173.
5. Apology to the Augsburg Confession, *Book of Concord*, page 169.
6. "The Third Article" in the Large Catechism, *Book of Concord*, page 416.
7. Gustaf Aulén, *The Faith of the Christian Church*, translated from the fifth Swedish edition by Eric H. Wahlstrom (Philadelphia: Muhlenberg, 1960), pages 294-295.
8. Kent S. Knutson, *Gospel, Church, Mission* (Minneapolis: Augsburg, 1976), page 56.
9. Muhlenberg, Volume 1, page 202.
10. Provision 4.01., ELCA churchwide constitution (2005 edition), page 21.
11. Provision 8.11., ELCA churchwide constitution (2005 edition), page 52.
12. Provision 5.01.c., ELCA churchwide constitution (2005 edition), page 23.
13. As used herein, *ecclesial* means "of or relating to church" (see Webster's Ninth New Collegiate Dictionary).
14. Provision 8.12., ELCA churchwide constitution (2005 edition), page 52.
15. Provision 8.13., ELCA churchwide constitution (2005 edition), page 52.
16. Provision 8.14., ELCA churchwide constitution (2005 edition), page 52.
17. Provision 8.17., ELCA churchwide constitution (2005 edition), page 52.
18. Provision 8.16., ELCA churchwide constitution (2005 edition), page 52.
19. Provision 8.15., ELCA churchwide constitution (2005 edition), page 52.
20. *C4.02. in the Model Constitution for Congregations of the Evangelical Lutheran Church in America. See also †S6.02. in the Constitution for Synods, and provision 4.02. in the ELCA churchwide constitution.

CHAPTER 8

1. J.N.D. Kelly, *Early Christian Doctrines* (New York: Harper & Row, Publishers, 1960), page 200.
2. Kelly, page 413.
3. First sentence of provision 5.01., ELCA churchwide constitution (2005 edition), page 23.
4. Second and third sentences of provision 5.01., ELCA churchwide constitution (2005 edition), page 23.
5. Provision 5.01.a., ELCA churchwide constitution (2005 edition), page 23.
6. Provision 6.01., ELCA churchwide constitution (2005 edition), page 26.
7. Provision 3.02., ELCA churchwide constitution (2005 edition), page 20. As printed herein, italic emphasis has been added. Further, this provision has been divided for greater clarity regarding the elements expressed within it.
8. Based on the author's personal notes. See also: Edgar R. Trexler, *Anatomy of a Merger* (Minneapolis: Augsburg, 1991), pages 165ff.
9. As ELCA churchwide constitution provision 5.01. says:
The Evangelical Lutheran Church in America shall be one church. This church recognizes that all power and authority in the Church belongs to the Lord Jesus Christ, its head. Therefore, all actions of this church by congregations, synods, and the churchwide organization shall be carried out under his rule and authority in accordance with the following principles:
a. The congregations, synods, and churchwide organization shall act in accordance with the Confession of Faith set forth in chapter 2 of this constitution and with the Statement of Purpose set forth in chapter 4.
b. This church, in faithfulness to the Gospel, is committed to be an inclusive church in the midst of division in society. Therefore, in their organization and outreach, the congregations, synods, and churchwide units of this church shall seek to exhibit the inclusive unity that is God's will for the Church.
c. The congregations, synods, and churchwide organization of this church are interdependent partners sharing responsibly in God's mission. In an interdependent relationship primary responsibility for particular functions will vary between the partners. Whenever possible, the entity most directly affected by a decision shall be the principal party responsible for decision and implementation, with the other entities facilitating

and assisting. Each congregation, synod, and separately incorporated unit of the churchwide organization, as well as the churchwide organization itself, is a separate legal entity and is responsible for exercising its powers and authorities.

d.   Each congregation and synod in its governing documents shall include the Confession of Faith and Statement of Purpose and such structural components as are required in this constitution. Beyond these common elements, congregations and synods shall be free to organize in such manner as each deems appropriate for its jurisdiction.

e.   The Church Council shall establish an ongoing process to review the function of the structural organization of this church and to develop recommendations for changes.

f.   Except as otherwise provided in this constitution and bylaws, the churchwide organization, through the Church Council, shall establish processes that will ensure that at least 60 percent of the members of its assemblies, councils, committees, boards, and other organizational units shall be laypersons; that as nearly as possible, 50 percent of the lay members of these assemblies, councils, committees, boards, or other organizational units shall be female and 50 percent shall be male, and that, where possible, the representation of ordained ministers shall be both female and male. At least ten percent of the members of these assemblies, councils, committees, boards, or other organizational units shall be persons of color and/or persons whose primary language is other than English. Processes shall be developed that will assure that in selecting staff there will be a balance of women and men, persons of color and persons whose primary language is other than English, laypersons, and persons on the roster of ordained ministers. This balance is to be evident in terms of both executive staff and support staff consistent with the inclusive policy of this church.

g.   Except as otherwise provided in this constitution and bylaws, synods, through synodical councils, shall establish processes that will ensure that at least 60 percent of the members of their assemblies, councils, committees, boards, and other organizational units shall be laypersons; that, as nearly as possible, 50 percent of the lay members of their assemblies, councils, committees, boards, or other organizational units shall be female and 50 percent shall be male, and that, where possible, the representation of ordained ministers shall be both female and male. Each synod shall establish processes that will enable it to reach a minimum goal that ten percent of the membership of its assemblies, councils, committees, boards, or other organizational units be persons of color and/or persons whose primary language is other than English.

h.   Leaders in this church should demonstrate that they are servants by their words, life-style, and manner of leadership. Leaders in this church will recognize their accountability to the Triune God, to the whole Church, to each other, and to the organization of this church in which they have been asked to serve.

i.   As a steward of the resources that God has provided, this church shall organize itself to make the most effective use of its resources to accomplish its mission.

j.   Each assembly, council, committee, board, commission, task force, or other body of the churchwide organization or any churchwide units shall be conclusively presumed to have been properly constituted, and neither the method of selection nor the composition of any such assembly, council, committee, board, commission, task force, or other body may be challenged in a court of law by any person or be used as the basis of a challenge in a court of law to the validity or effect of any action taken or authorized by any such assembly, council, committee, board, commission, task force, or other body.

10. As provided in chapter 6 of the ELCA churchwide constitution on "Membership":

6.01.   The members of this church shall be the baptized members of its congregations.

6.02.   The voting members of this church shall be those persons elected to serve as members of the Churchwide Assembly. Membership in a congregation does not, in itself, confer voting rights in this corporation.

11. As provided in chapter 7 of the ELCA churchwide constitution on "Ministry":

7.11.   This church affirms the universal priesthood of all its baptized members. In its function and its structure this church commits itself to the equipping and supporting of all its members for their ministries in the world and in this church. It is within this context of ministry that this church calls some of its baptized members for specific ministries in this church.

7.21. Within the people of God and for the sake of the Gospel ministry entrusted to all believers, God has instituted the office of ministry of Word and sacrament. To carry out this ministry, this church calls and ordains qualified persons.

7.22. A pastor as an ordained minister of this church shall be a person whose commitment to Christ, soundness in the faith, aptness to preach, teach, and witness, and educational qualifications have been examined and approved in the manner prescribed in the documents of this church; who has been properly called and ordained; who accepts and adheres to the Confession of Faith of this church; who is diligent and faithful in the exercise of the ministry; and whose life and conduct are above reproach. A minister shall comply with the constitution of this church.

12. As provided in chapter 8 of the ELCA churchwide constitution on "Relationships":

8.11. This church shall seek to function as people of God through congregations, synods, and the churchwide organization, all of which shall be interdependent. Each part, while fully the church, recognizes that it is not the whole church and therefore lives in a partnership relationship with the others.

8.16. In faithful participation in the mission of God in and through this church, congregations, synods, and the churchwide organization—as interdependent expressions of this church—shall be guided by the biblical and confessional commitments of this church. Each shall recognize that mission efforts must be shaped by both local needs and global awareness, by both individual witness and corporate endeavor, and by both distinctly Lutheran emphases and growing ecumenical cooperation.

13. As provided in chapter 9 of the ELCA churchwide constitution on "Congregations":

9.11. A congregation is a community of baptized persons whose existence depends on the proclamation of the Gospel and the administration of the sacraments and whose purpose is to worship God, to nurture its members, and to reach out in witness and service to the world. To this end it assembles regularly for worship and nurture, organizes and carries out ministry to its people and neighborhood, and cooperates with and supports the wider church to strive for the fulfillment of God's mission in the world.

9.20.   Criteria for Recognition and Reception

9.21.   This church shall recognize, receive, and maintain on the roster those congregations which by their practice as well as their governing documents:

    a.   preach the Word, administer the sacraments, and carry out God's mission;

    b.   accept this church's Confession of Faith;

    c.   agree to the Statement of Purpose of this church;

    d.   agree to call pastoral leadership from the clergy roster of this church in accordance with the call procedures of this church except in special circumstances and with the approval of the synodical bishop;

    e.   agree to be responsible for their life as a Christian community; and

    f.   agree to support the life and work of this church.

14.   As provided in chapter 10 of the ELCA churchwide constitution on "Synods":

    10.21.   Each synod, in partnership with the churchwide organization, shall bear primary responsibility for the oversight of the life and mission of this church in its territory. . . .

15.   As provided in chapter 11 of the ELCA churchwide constitution on the "Churchwide Organization":

    11.11.   The Evangelical Lutheran Church in America shall have a churchwide organization that shall function interdependently with the congregations and synods of this church. The churchwide organization shall serve on behalf of and in support of this church's members, congregations, and synods in proclaiming the Gospel, reaching out in witness and service both globally and throughout the territory of this church, nurturing the members of this church in the daily life of faith, and manifesting the unity of this church with the whole Church of Jesus Christ.

16.   Carl E. Braaten, *Principles of Lutheran Theology* (Philadelphia: Fortress, 1983), pages 50 and 52.

17.   THE AMERICAN LUTHERAN CHURCH: The American Lutheran Church (ALC), formed in 1960, used the following definition of membership: "The membership of The American Lutheran Church shall consist of congregations. The requirements for membership shall be: a. The profession of a common faith. b. The acceptance of this Constitution and its Bylaws. c. Participation on the program of activity approved by this Church" (Provision 6.11. in the Constitution and Bylaws of The American Lutheran Church). Likewise, in the ALC

district constitution, this definition was provided: "The membership of the district shall be composed of congregations" (D5.10. in the District Constitution). Further, the following was stipulated in ALC provision 4.13.: Congregations . . . pledge themselves to assure . . . [the ALC] the human authority, power, and resources needed to carry out its purpose as set forth in this Constitution. The American Lutheran Church pledges itself to use its authority, power, and resources both to serve its congregations directly and to serve their interests in those spheres where congregations cannot act effectively alone. . . ." Strictly speaking, neither the districts nor the national office of The American Lutheran Church were seen as possessing any legitimate ecclesial (i.e., churchly) character in themselves. Their functions were only delegated ones from congregations. Only congregations were seen as "church," as reflected in The American Lutheran Church's constitution and bylaws. As a further indication of this understanding, the word *pastor* was defined and restricted to "a member of the clergy serving a parish" (ALC bylaw 7.22.12.).

LUTHERAN CHURCH IN AMERICA: By contrast, the membership of the Lutheran Church in America (LCA), formed in 1962, was defined in this way: "This church shall consist . . . of the congregations and ordained ministers . . ." (Article III, Section 1 of the Constitution of the Lutheran Church in America). Further, it was provided that: "Congregations and ordained ministers when organized into a synod may through such synod unite with this church upon application for membership, subscription to this constitution including its Confession of Faith, and acceptance . . . at a convention of this church" (Article III, Section 3 of the LCA constitution). The definition of the Lutheran Church in America "was heavily influenced by Henry Melchior Muhlenberg, who called together Lutheran clergy and lay people to found the Ministerium of Pennsylvania in 1748. The former United Lutheran Church in America continued this focus and it was reinforced by the former Augustana Lutheran Church when the LCA was formed . . . ," Edgar R. Trexler has written (see *Anatomy of a Merger*, page 167).

ASSOCIATION OF EVANGELICAL LUTHERAN CHURCHES: The Association of Evangelical Lutheran Churches (AELC), formed in 1976 in a separation from The Lutheran Church–Missouri Synod (LCMS), defined itself less as a church body and more as a free association. This both carried forward the strong congregational polity of the LCMS and also reflected the turmoil out of which the AELC was formed. That turmoil led to strong suspicions of vesting any authority anywhere other than in each congregation alone.

18. Large Catechism, *Book of Concord*, page 416.

19. Aulén, pages 312-317.

20. Large Catechism, *Book of Concord*, pages 417-418.

21. Conrad Bergendoff, "Church," *The Encyclopedia of the Lutheran Church*, Volume 1, Julius Bodensieck, editor (Minneapolis: Augsburg, 1965), page 487.

CHAPTER 9

1. As stated in the Apology to the Augsburg Confession, "The church has the command to appoint ministers; to this we must subscribe wholeheartedly, for we know that God approves this ministry and is present in it. It is good to extol the ministry of the Word with every possible kind of praise in opposition to the fanatics who dream that the Holy Spirit does not come through the Word but because of their own preparations" (*Book of Concord*, pages 212-213).

2. Abdel Ross Wentz, *The Lutheran Church in American History* (Philadelphia: United Lutheran Publishing House, 1933), page 312.

3. S. Anita Stauffer, "Christian Worship: Toward Localization and Globalization," *Worship and Culture in Dialogue* (Geneva: Lutheran World Federation, 1994), pages 11-12.

4. Stauffer, pages 14-15.

5. Abdel Ross Wentz, *A Basic History of Lutheranism in America* (Philadelphia: Muhlenberg Press, 1955), page 186.

6. Provision 5.01.h., ELCA churchwide constitution (2005 edition), page 24.

7. Provision 5.01.i., ELCA churchwide constitution (2005 edition), page 24.

CHAPTER 10

1. Sabine Baring-Gould, "Onward, Christian Soldiers," *The Concordia Hymnal* (Minneapolis: Augsburg, 1932), page 374.

2. Hefner, "Basic Elements of the Church's Life," *Christian Dogmatics*, page 223.

3. Herman A. Preus, *A Theology to Live By: The Practical Luther for the Practicing Christian* (St. Louis: Concordia, 1977), page 34.

4. Hefner, "Basic Elements of the Church's Life," *Christian Dogmatics*, page 236.

5. Hefner, "The Being of the Church," *Christian Dogmatics*, pages 210-211.